# Extreme Day Trips in Europe

## A guide to booking and enjoying a day trip abroad

Sarah Deeks

Copyright © 2024 Sarah Deeks

All rights reserved.

ISBN: 9798875600548

# TABLE OF CONTENTS

Acknowledgements ........................................................................... 4

Introduction ..................................................................................... 5

Part One: Practical Matters ............................................................ 17

    Passports: the essential documents ................................................. 18

    Travel insurance (including the EHIC and GHIC card) ...................... 18

    Spending money .............................................................................. 19

    Which bag to bring .......................................................................... 21

    When to book your flights or Eurostar train tickets ......................... 22

    Where to go? ................................................................................... 24

    Searching by preferred destination .................................................. 24

    Choosing the most suitable flight times ........................................... 25

    Searching by departure airport ........................................................ 26

    Book directly with the airline, not through a flight finder site ......... 27

    Extend your trip cheaply: fly in and out of different destinations and sleep on the move ............................................................................ 28

    Multi-country trip suggestions ......................................................... 29

    Beware of extra charges .................................................................. 29

    Booking same-day flights at the airport (or not) .............................. 30

    Travelling by Eurostar train ............................................................. 31

    Arriving at your departure airport ................................................... 31

    Options for travel to your departure airport .................................... 33

    Driving and parking ......................................................................... 33

    Drop off and collection by a friend or family member ..................... 34

    Public transport ............................................................................... 34

Airport taxis ...................................................................................... 35
Enjoy the journey .............................................................................. 35
Coping with tiredness ....................................................................... 36
Is extreme travel doable with children? .......................................... 37
Local navigation of your chosen destination .................................. 39
Map Apps ........................................................................................... 39
Downloading maps to use offline .................................................... 41
Asking locals for help with directions .............................................. 42
If things go wrong .............................................................................. 43
Personal security and scams ............................................................ 43
Medical attention .............................................................................. 45
Delayed or cancelled flights home .................................................. 45

# Part Two: Destination Guides ......................................................... 47

# Northern Europe ............................................................................... 51

England ................................................................................................ 51
Scotland ............................................................................................... 56
Wales .................................................................................................... 59
Northern Ireland ................................................................................. 62
Republic of Ireland ............................................................................. 65
Denmark .............................................................................................. 69
Sweden ................................................................................................ 74
Finland ................................................................................................. 77
Norway ................................................................................................ 80
Iceland ................................................................................................. 82

# Western Europe ................................................................................. 84

France .................................................................................................. 84

Belgium ................................................................................. 98

The Netherlands .................................................................. 104

**Eastern Europe** ................................................................... **111**

Hungary ............................................................................. 111

Slovakia .............................................................................. 113

Bratislava ........................................................................... 113

Czechia (Czech Republic) ................................................... 115

Romania ............................................................................. 117

**Southern Europe** ................................................................ **119**

Spain .................................................................................. 119

Italy .................................................................................... 130

Portugal ............................................................................. 139

Albania .............................................................................. 143

**Central Europe** ................................................................... **146**

Switzerland ........................................................................ 146

Germany ............................................................................ 153

Austria ............................................................................... 167

Poland ................................................................................ 171

Slovenia ............................................................................. 175

**Part Three: 50 Bonus Travel Tips** .................................... **177**

**Conclusion** ........................................................................... **188**

**A Note from the Author** .................................................... **192**

# Acknowledgements

A huge thank you to the members (and in particular, the founders) of the 'Extreme Travel UK' Facebook group. It was this group and its multitude of inspiring trip reviews that opened my eyes to the potential to enjoy international day trips within Europe.

# Introduction

Perhaps you were intrigued by the title of this book and the unfamiliar notion of 'Extreme Day Trips' which prompted you to pick it up and discover more?

What exactly are 'Extreme Day Trips'? I am glad you asked. 'Extreme Day Tripping' (sometimes shortened to 'EDT') is a recent term coined by British travellers who thrive on the challenge of researching, booking and then spending a single day travelling to and back from a destination in a foreign country. At a push, should flight times or other reasons render the return leg impossible on the same day then they may return the following day. The general idea though is that an EDT is a micro trip. A condensed holiday of sorts, with all the usual sense of excitement and anticipation of exploring a new place and sampling the best it has to offer but *without* incurring the higher costs and committing to the extra days that longer trips require.

You would be forgiven for believing the traditional trope that jaunts abroad must be booked months in advance and are only worth doing if you can spare multiple days and plenty of cash to splash on a trip. This book aims to shake up these outdated notions about travel, certainly within Europe, and open your eyes to the fact that travel can be just as meaningful and fun when booked merely weeks (or even days) ahead and in a condensed timescale. Perhaps even more so.

## Why go on an Extreme Day Trip?

To those hearing about the concept for the first time, it may sound an impracticable and slightly ridiculous one as by nature it generally involves a very early start and late finish to the day. So why on earth would you contemplate an EDT yourself? There are many reasons and one or more of the below may resonate with you. They primarily tend to involve either a lack of money or a lack of time.

The cost-of-living crisis has impacted the personal finances of a large swathe of society. Thousands of individuals who could previously stretch to a couple of holidays or few short breaks each year have been forced to slash their spending on travel and leisure. In this challenging era of rising living costs, there may seem to be no option other than to shelve our dreams of foreign travel. For others who have yet to experience their first time abroad on a plane or leave their birth country, the very prospect of doing so may seem to be sliding further and further out of reach. But rethinking the idea that a trip abroad necessitates multiple consecutive days away and instead is doable in a single day or as an overnighter can be a game changer. Eliminating the need for accommodation shaves off a significant portion of a trip abroad cost (indeed accommodation is often the most cost-sucking element of a holiday budget). Without pricey accommodation to factor into a trip it is surprising how affordable a jaunt away can be. It is not unusual to be able to pick up a return flight to an exotic-sounding continental city for less than the price of a one-way train ticket from London to Birmingham.

EDTs offer an ideal mode of travel to those for whom time, or rather a lack of it, is the main barrier. For a multitude of reasons people may be unable to take a multi-day break. This could be down to the demands of work, or perhaps caring responsibilities rule out the possibility of taking off for more than a day or so. Conversely, perhaps you are someone who quickly finds themself getting itchy feet and bored in the same place once the top attractions have been checked out and ticked off within a few short hours. Others may lack the headspace to plan enough to stay occupied for a string of days in an unfamiliar location and would prefer to simply select a couple of highlights or stroll around somewhere new for a complete change of scene and enjoy the mood-boosting effects that doing so brings. Some of us simply view ourselves as homebirds who prefer to be tucked up in our own familiar bed every night. There are as many reasons as there are people.

**Are many people already taking return trips abroad in a single day?**

Yes. In fact, thousands of people have already caught on to the benefits of this type of micro-travel and are taking full advantage of it. Social media groups exist for the sole purpose of committed EDT fans sharing their inspiring trip reviews and supporting each other with trip planning.

Although an easy fact to take for granted, those who are lucky enough to live in Europe (either on the geographical mainland or in the British or other isles) or happen to be visiting a European country for an extended stay, are in a uniquely blessed position to have proximity to scores of separate nations, the majority of which can be visited in a single day. Each of these possess their own distinct culture, language, long and eventful history and resulting iconic landmarks to be discovered. As an added bonus, much of Europe has extensive public transportation systems that are generally clean, efficient and affordable which facilitates easy transfers from the destination airport to the heart of the city.

Recent UK newspaper articles have raised awareness of the possibilities of EDTs. One memorable story featured a group of mothers who jetted from their homes near London to a great value yet renowned luxury spa in Italy for a bit of pampering, then arrived back in time to tuck their children into bed. Countless other individuals with a particular passion think nothing of hopping onto a plane for a couple of hours to indulge in their hobby with a bunch of like-minded people. International cheese shows, Swiss watch-making conventions, robotics conferences, you name it. Many events tend to be held in central European countries to facilitate easy access for attendees from surrounding countries. Return travel home at the end of the day is (understandably) preferable to attempting to book an overpriced local hotel while such events are being held. Music fans offer a further example: devotees of musical artists have no hesitation in booking a flight to watch their idol perform at a daytime festival or evening concert, staying overnight if unavoidable but then they catch the first flight home the next morning.

Maybe you know friends or family members who have moved away to another European country and until now thought you could never spare the funds or time to visit them. An EDT would enable you to schedule a meet-up in their closest city for a leisurely lunch, long chat and the chance to see a little of their locality. Could the prospect spur you on to finally book that overdue catchup?

**Is an EDT worth the effort?**

The answer to this question, on behalf the many thousands of people who are already converts to the EDT movement is a resounding 'yes'. You may have doubts about the practicalities of return travel in a single day or fear that friends and family would express incredulity for you even considering it. That is understandable: doubts are natural but in the coming pages you will be guided through the logistics of planning and executing your first extreme trip as well as presented the visitor attractions that dozens of destinations have to offer. Chances are that you will become so convinced of the benefits that you will catch the EDT bug yourself. If you encounter critics or find that others express their incredulity, you can smile sweetly knowing that they are the ones missing out on (quite literally) the world.

One fact that goes over the heads of EDT critics is that the challenge of maximising the experience and pleasure within a limited time frame forms an intrinsic part of the appeal of express day trips. Converts to the movement can testify to the buzz it brings. Rising with the lark is a piece of cake when you know that instead of a day in the office you are destined for zooming across the continent. Starting your day early is a vital tool of the extreme day tripper: it serves to stretch out the day and carves out extra scope for exploring a destination. You can take pleasure in knowing that you are in the virtual company of thousands of others in the EDT community heading to their local airport on any given morning, each looking forward to checking out the charming places of interest on their must-see list and wondering what little details about the quirks and customs of their destined country they will observe. The ethereal sense of manipulating time and stretching out the day by beginning it early, ending it late and experiencing so much in the hours between feels a little magical.

Critics who contend that an international day trip is not worth the effort are likely to be fortunate enough to have bags of time and money to devote to exploring our remarkable planet. That's great for them. The rest of us, getting by on limited budgets of both funds and time, must snatch whatever opportunities we can to get out there and see the world with both hands. We have probably all heard snooty assertions that cities such as Paris must be visited for days or weeks on end to even scratch the surface of her extensive cultural offerings. Yet as a longtime lover of Paris who has 'only' visited a few times for 1-3 day stretches, I personally find that remaining conscious of the fact that each visit will be fleeting spurs me on to make the most of every minute. I cherry-pick the experiences that most encapsulate the essence of Paris to me whilst mindfully absorbing her charm and atmosphere. You absolutely can, too.

Removing oneself physically far away from what can too often feel a humdrum existence and escaping the stresses of everyday life for just one day can be sufficient to shift our perspective on life, prompt creative ideas and renew our joie de vivre. Have you ever visited a foreign country and marvelled at something unique to that destination? Perhaps a beautiful local handicraft that you could not resist purchasing to display in your home and admire for years to come (and serve as a memento of the trip)? Or just one taste of a delicious regional delicacy inspired you to search for authentic recipes back home to recreate the experience and so prolong the pleasure? The melodic accents of a foreign language may have motivated you to begin learning a little of it yourself. _The experience of a single day away really can bring about lasting change to your life.

There is also an undeniable thrill to sliding under the covers of your very own bed in your familiar home, physically exhausted but mentally buzzing while marvelling at the incredible modern feat that has enabled you to be transported hundreds of miles since that morning. Do not be surprised if you experience the giddy sensation of feeling as though you must have spent significantly more time away than the scant few hours that you have. Fresh memories of having had all your senses stimulated through observing life being played out in a new-to-your-eyes place will whirl through your mind as you close your eyes to rest. Indeed, being able to experience all of this in under 24 hours *should* feel like modern-day miracle. Folk from a single century ago would surely have scoffed at such an unlikely occurrence being possible. It is also important to remember how privileged we are that it is financially and geographically possible for ordinary folk in Europe to traverse to a multitude of different countries within the boundaries of a single day or so.

### Are long day trips a new phenomenon?

Long day trips per se are not in fact a new phenomenon, even if the destinations have become increasingly exotic over time. Only a few generations ago for masses of ordinary, working-class Brits, the closest they ever would have experienced to today's definition of a holiday was probably an annual day trip to a quintessential resort on the nearest coastline to their home. That one, eagerly anticipated family day trip to the seaside often necessitated an early start in the morning to facilitate preparations such as making sandwiches for the entire family's lunch as well as drinks and snacks. They would then make their way (often on foot) to the bus or railway station. Back then transport was slower, making for longer journey times. On reaching their destination, the day would consist of simple pleasures such as building sandcastles, paddling at the shore's edge, watching a Punch and Judy puppet show, strolling around and generally enjoying the jovial atmosphere. Come midday they would tuck into their picnic lunches and if sufficiently flush, splash out on an ice cream. Before long, it would be time to hurry back for the train or bus home. Many folk today would shake their heads in wonder that it seemed worth the mammoth effort of waking up early, having to prepare and cart around their own lunch for the day, sitting for extended periods on a (likely uncomfortable) train or bus just for a few hours of basic entertainment less than eighty miles maximum from the home. Yet clearly hordes of people did, as the plentiful photographic evidence of thriving Great British Victorian seaside resorts can testify.

I cannot help but feel that the surge in popularity of EDTs is a modern-day version of those seaside day trips of the past. Is it not a natural human yearning to venture and explore beyond the little pocket of the world that is our hometown? To crave a change of scene and taste what else the world has to offer beyond the monotonous daily routines that embody our lives?

## Is it easy for an inexperienced traveller to figure out the logistics?

EDTs are ideal for those wanting to dip their toe in the water and experience other countries and cultures. The 'Practical Matters' section aims to explain everything clearly to those who are unfamiliar with air travel. By the time you have finished reading this book, I hope you will be fired up to book your first day trip or overnight trip abroad, confident that you have the know-how to go about doing so. Take your pick from some of the most fascinating cultures and historic cities in the world, as little as an hour's flight away.

I hope the section on destination guides whets your appetite for potential sights and attractions on offer in some of the most accessible cities from the United Kingdom (as well as from other European countries). However, resist the temptation to design an itinerary overly crammed with attractions. Particularly for your first day trip when you will be adjusting to an earlier than usual start to your day as well as needing to navigate airports and unfamiliar surroundings, simplicity is best. Many travellers report that they happened to stumble across hidden gems and extracted the essence of a place just by strolling around the historic central streets. Taking a little time out to people watch over a cup of coffee in a café rarely disappoints, also. Leave yourself open to surprise opportunities that may unfold around a literal corner: you might even stumble upon a free live concert, parade or festival. There is always the option of returning to a city should you feel there is much remaining to be explored.

**How to use this book**

This is a book of three distinct parts.

The first section, **'Practical Matters'** intends to act as a guide for those who may be inexperienced in international travel and navigating airports and/ or feel overwhelmed at the prospect of researching and booking flights. It also serves to act as a guide for those who are new to searching for and booking single day trips abroad and need to learn the most effective ways of finding the best flights. There is also plenty of information on other practical matters to give thought to when travelling abroad - from the most cost-effective ways of spending money and sleeping on the move to navigating your way around an unfamiliar city.

The second section is titled: **'Destination Guides'**. It features an extensive selection of destinations (well over 50) including most European capital cities, that can be flown to on low cost airlines from UK airports (as well as from other European destinations). Depending on your local airport, a decent number of them should be within your reach as single day trips, or at least overnighters. Each city guide includes a selection of the most interesting places of interest plus often a few lesser-known gems. There should be something to appeal to the tastes of most visitors in each guide. Importantly, each one also includes details on how to access the city centre from the airport served by budget airlines from the UK.

This book is not intended to (and without becoming an unwieldly large size could not) be an exhaustive guide to every possible European destination that can be flown to from the UK. Undoubtedly, you will be fortunate enough to find that numerous other, unlisted destinations are available as options to visit which I hope you will enjoy researching and exploring.

The final section is '**50 Bonus Travel Tips**', featuring a mix of practical hacks and budget-saving ideas intended to help you squeeze the maximum value and experience from your trips.

Does all this sound fascinating, if a little daunting? The information that follows will equip you with all you need to book a bargain-priced flight and be in possession of every scrap of knowledge required to design your first micro trip. Adopt the relaxed, take-it-as-it comes approach of strolling around your first destination to see what takes your fancy on arrival or curate a personalised itinerary to include what you deem to be the must-see landmarks and attractions; the choice is yours.

# Part One: Practical Matters

## Practical Matters

While jetting off for a day or so need not be daunting in terms of the practicalities, should you have little experience of international travel you may be glad of an outline of the basic aspects to consider in advance to ensure a smooth trip.

### Passports: the essential documents

If you possess a passport, that is the critical document ticked off already. If not, apply for one as soon as possible as at peak processing times that all-important document can take weeks or even months to arrive. If you already hold a passport double check it is still in date (obvious but important) with 3-6 months' validity past the intended date of travel (the rules vary by destination country). More specifically, note that if the expiry date is later than 10 years to the day of the start date, the passport will expire sooner than the printed end date: it will expire 10 years to the exact day of the start date. Despite being common knowledge to many owing to media coverage, travellers get turned away every week in the UK due to not realising about this Brexit change rendering UK passport 'added months' no longer valid.

## Travel insurance (including the EHIC and GHIC card)

It is best not to skimp on this, for healthcare provision if nothing else and the good news is that cover for a day or two is as cheap as chips. If you only intend to go for one or two extreme trips a year then day cover each time works out as better value, but if you travel abroad multiple times a year then annual policies make better financial sense. Bring along your policy certificate with the emergency telephone number on your travels.

Equally importantly for healthcare cover (but often forgotten about) is the UK GHIC (UK Global Health Insurance Card) and UK EHIC (UK European Health Insurance Card). The latter card has been phased out in recent years but is fine to use until its expiry date, approaching which you should apply for the newer GHIC card. The GHIC card is free to apply for via the official website (though beware of unofficial sites that charge an unnecessary £10 or more administration fee) at services.nhsbsa.nhs.uk/cra/start.

Both cards enable you to benefit from state-provided healthcare for emergency treatment abroad at the same price a local would access it for (anything from free upwards). Although the need will hopefully never arise for any treatment, this card should be presented alongside paid-for travel health insurance details on arrival at a hospital or health centre.

## Spending money

Although cash payments may be on the decline in favour of credit card payments in parts of Europe, this is not the case throughout the whole continent. For the far northern nations of Sweden, Denmark, Norway, Finland and Iceland card payments are preferred and -in some instances - the only payment option available. However, it is wise to bring along the equivalent of £50 in the local currency to cover the cost an unanticipated taxi ride back to the airport for instance, or to cover other unexpected spends. Regardless of the specific local currency, Euros are widely accepted as payment in a number of eastern European nations (though you will probably be handed back local currency as change in non-Euro countries such as Albania).

Most large towns and cities will have ATM machines situated outside banks. These are convenient for withdrawing cash if needed, but charges will apply to each withdrawal.

Should you make purchases on a debit or credit card directly on a card reader machine and the option flashes up to pay in either your home currency or the local currency, selecting the latter option is usually more cost effective. It is worth researching the best credit card providers a few weeks before any planed travels abroad to apply for one that promises minimal or even zero fees when withdrawing money or paying on a card reader internationally.

A prepaid travel card or a currency card such as Fair FX can be a savvy choice for spending abroad because its exchange rates tend to be more favourable. You can load your chosen currency on to it before you leave then spend it on abroad like a normal debit card.

Generally, I travel with two payment cards, each from separate banks because if one of them fails to work abroad then the other one usually does. On occasions, card payments have been declined when I attempted to make contactless payments then subsequently worked fine when inserting it into the card reader instead, so I usually insert my card into the card reader as a matter of course at ticket machines etc.

**Which bag to bring**

The optimal choice is the smallest one you can manage with. One of the best parts about short trips is the ability to travel light. Bear in mind that whatever you choose to take with you, you will have to lug around all day. For an international day trip, a small, lightweight backpack often comes in useful. A thin raincoat or pack-a-mac is a good idea in case of rain showers.

For an overnight trip a few more essentials will obviously be required and therefore necessitates a larger bag. To avoid needing to pay extra for a cabin bag, plump for one of the bag types that fit neatly under the seat in front of you. The maximum dimensions for such a bag on most budget airlines are 40cm x 25cm x 20cm. This could include a handbag or laptop type bag. An internet search for 'cabin bag 40x20x25cm' should generate a list of many possible bags to purchase within the permitted size limit. Fortunately, this size of bag is generous enough to fit a night or two's clothing and other essentials in. Backpack-style bags with two shoulder straps tend to feel most comfortable for a full day's lugging around due to the design providing even weight distribution.

At the time of writing, liquids must be in containers of 100ml or less when you pass through airport security and these need to be placed in a single transparent, resealable bag of maximum size 20x20cm. Drinking bottles need to be emptied out at security but can be refilled once through or alternatively a bottle of water can easily be purchased from the airside shops. In fact, a single carrier bag containing items purchased airside can be brought on board in addition to your hand baggage allowance which means that picking up toiletries once through Security can be a clever way to boost your baggage allowance when packing for a stayover trip- although need to be carried around with you all day which could prove a hassle.

**When to book your flights or Eurostar train tickets**

Booking a few months in advance generally boosts your chances of snapping up seats at the lowest price. However, avoid booking on an airline's new season release day because the associated hype pushes up demand and thus prices rise in turn. About a fortnight after release days the prices should be better value. That said, trips abroad need not be planned many months in advance - in fact, bargains are often to be found relatively last minute in term time when demand is lower as airlines prefer to fly their planes at maximum passenger capacity. They figure that if they have guaranteed customers in seats, even if sold at cost price, those customers may spend extra on in-flight food, duty free goods etc. A quick search on an airline's website will reveal that there often seems to be a 'sweet spot' for low priced tickets being sold 4-5 weeks before departure. In off-peak season, it is not unheard of to see flight prices drop weeks or even days before departure if the airline has not sold enough seats, particularly to less popular destinations such as Tirana and Sofia. If you do snap up a last-minute bargain flight ticket, rest assured that there will still be ample time to buy travel insurance and research the key sights and experiences at your destination that take your fancy.

Eurostar sell special offer seats (the lowest ones tend to be £39 one-way) in regular promotional sales. Sign up for their marketing emails to receive alerts of when these are about to occur. Regardless of these sales, Eurostar follows a similar supply and demand pattern to airlines in that the lowest seat prices are to be found midweek in school term time and between September and the end of June.

**Where to go?**

**Searching by preferred destination**

Should you have a hankering to visit a particular location, then your best bet is to search for it on flight finder sites. The two best known of these are Skyscanner.com and GoogleFlights.com websites. Both work wonders at identifying cheap flights but operate in slightly different ways so there is no harm in searching on them both. Skyscanner also has an app version, though user feedback indicates that the website version is superior for search options as well as for highlighting the cheapest possible seats.

There are less established flight finder sites that show promise to search at least as well, if not better that are worth checking out, too. These include Azair.com which offers some useful advanced search features such as searching effectively even with vague destination criteria e.g. 'Greek islands' or 'Mediterranean coast' or a loose time period e.g. 'in July or August'. Kiwi.com is another strong contender: as on the other fledgling site Azair.com you can easily identify flight options from multiple airports for return day trips in a single search rather than carry out a separate search for each departure airport.

Simply type in your preferred departure airport(s) and arrival city on your flight finder site of choice and then scan the results. Be sure to tick the box next to 'direct flights' underneath the main search details, too (on a day or overnight trip time is too precious a resource to waste on flight stops).

Should the results not yield any suitable flight results, it is worth casting your eyes over a map of the desired destination for nearby large cities that could well be served by an airport (note that the aeroplane symbol is commonly used to indicate the location of airports on maps). Even airports over the border of other countries could be viable options. For instance, a great many people routinely fly into Denmark's Copenhagen airport to access southern Sweden; for many Swedes Copenhagen is the airport of choice for all air travel. Do then check that transport links from any potential airport make your preferred destination a realistic option. Excellent rail networks that run from European airports and between cities as well as extensive route coverage by coach companies such as Flixbus.com could make it surprisingly feasible. Rome2rio.com is a useful site to check out your transport options between two locations for this purpose.

**Choosing the most suitable flight times**

Where airlines offer multiple flights on the same day to a destination, they will usually be priced differently, according to demand. Although snapping up a bargain priced flight is always pleasing, the primary consideration for a day trip abroad should be the flight timings. To maximise what can be seen and experienced in a short time frame, the first flight of the day usually makes the most sense. This tends to be from around 06:00am onwards as the earliest departures are intended to cater to business travellers needing to arrive at their foreign city at the start of the business day.

Sometimes there will only be one available flight per day (if that- less popular routes may only be scheduled a few times a week). Depending on the return flight time (if any) this may render a day trip impossible. No need to give up at the first hurdle, though. A bit of creative thinking could resolve the issue. Should you be able to spare an extra day (even just an extra evening) and modest extra funds, you could turn the day trip into an overnighter (assuming that there is a return flight the preceding or following day).

Flying in to and out of different airports can also work well; I have booked a trip to Milan then flown into Milan Malpensa airport and back home from Milan Bergamo airport simply because I preferred the flight time home from Bergamo (despite there also being an evening return flight back from Malpensa).

## Searching by departure airport

Perhaps you are open to any destination and indeed, the prospect of scoring a ridiculously cheap ticket to a 'surprise' location holds a strong attraction? In that case, simply search on a flight finder site such as Sky Scanner for your most convenient departure airport and a potential date then select the 'explore everywhere' option that appears when you click in the 'to' box. As above, do tick the box next to the 'direct flights' underneath the main search boxes, too. When the search results are displayed, you will see country names listed in price ascending order. When you spot one that interests you just click on it to reveal a list of destination cities within that country (again, in price ascending order). Scroll down to peruse the various flights on offer.

The differences in price according to the various airlines will be noticeable, as will the fact that flights at more sociable times of the day tend to be more popular and thus priced higher. Fortunately, flights at extreme ends of the day are often priced at the lower end of the spectrum which works out favourably for day-trippers.

## Book directly with the airline, not through a flight finder site

Once you have identified the best flights and are ready to go ahead and book, it is strongly recommended that you do not click through the link on the flight finder site to book it, but instead head for the relevant airline's own website or app. This is because booking through flight finder sites such as Skyscanner and Google Flights often means you inadvertently book with an Online Travel Agency (OTA) which can make the flight check-in process a little more complicated than it needs to be and adds an extra layer of complication should you need to amend your flights.

**Extend your trip cheaply: fly in and out of different destinations and sleep on the move**

Should you wish to extend your stay from a day trip to an overnight or weekend trip, consider flying into one destination airport and back from a different one the following day or so. Should there be a neighbouring country of interest it makes sense to tag on a second destination for the next day. Doing so should be straightforward because as previously stated, continental Europe is served well by rail networks as well as widespread bus routes, primarily by the company 'Flixbus'.

To give one example, after exploring Berlin in Germany for the day you could catch a Flixbus overnight coach to Warsaw in Poland. If booked at least a couple of weeks in advance the cost could be as little as £30 for a relatively comfortable, reclining seat to rest in for the eight hour journey. Then, wake up in Warsaw with the day ahead to explore before flying home from Warsaw airport. It can work out as excellent value compared to shelling out for a hotel room and by sleeping on the move between cities (and often countries) you maximise sightseeing time. It is strongly advisable to reserve a seat in advance for the best value tickets as well as to guarantee a seat.

Night trains present an alternative way to travel long distances across the continent. Although pricier than coaches, they offer more comfort as narrow beds are often available for additional cost.

Should night travel not sound a good choice for you, there is always the option of spending the night in a hotel or a (more budget-friendly) hostel before taking a short train or coach ride to another country.

**Multi-country trip suggestions**

Here is a list of potential multi-destination trip combos that work well due to the shared borders and associated shorter times to reach each another by public transport.
- Denmark and Sweden
- Germany and Switzerland
- Belgium and the Netherlands
- Spain and Gibraltar
- Austria and Czechia (Czech Republic)
- Hungary and Slovakia
- Italy and Slovenia
- France and Belgium

- Estonia and Finland

**Beware of extra charges**

Beware of optional flight add-ons such as guaranteed seats together for travel companions, extra baggage allowance (almost always unnecessary for day trips or overnighters), in-flight meals as well as insurance options that all flash up during the booking process. Check carefully that you do not accidentally opt in to any of these.

Most budget airlines charge an additional fee for travel companions to be seated together. Should this be important, you need to pay extra for the privilege or take the gamble of their allocated seating systems (which from anecdotal evidence seems to sit passengers on the same booking as far away from each other as possible). On early EDT flights it often makes sense to catch a bit of extra sleep rather than chat!

**Booking same-day flights at the airport (or not)**

An urban myth is perpetuated that there are bargain flights to be had for those who spontaneously pack a bag and turning up at the airport in anticipation of flying somewhere the same day. Sadly, if this was ever a thing then it died out decades ago. Many airlines do not even have the capacity to sell flights at the airport desks and at those that do, the staff have been known to encourage potential customers to pull out their phones to book online for the best deal. Last minute flights are usually priced steeply by airlines for the simple reason that they know unsold flights for imminent departures will be snapped up by travellers who are left with no choice but to book them for specific reasons such as business travel, family emergencies etc.

**Travelling by Eurostar train**

This book primarily focuses on flying to destinations due to air travel being accessible to people in more geographical areas and a far wider range of destinations being visitable in a day. However, do not discount travel by train on the Eurostar, at least if you are fortunate enough to live close to London for the St Pancras terminal. High-speed trains operate direct services to several European cities that are close enough for a day trip, including: Paris, Brussels, Amsterdam, Lille and Lyon. Furthermore, bear in mind that rail connections from these major stations facilitate access to other cities and towns that you may have in mind to visit. All the information you need to research your options for travelling on Eurostar can be found on seat61.com.

**Arriving at your departure airport**

Bear in mind that passengers are generally advised to arrive at the airport two hours before the flight departure time to be sure of clearing security at busier times. Outside of peak season, this could potentially be reduced to ninety minutes (or whatever you feel comfortable with) and even less for smaller airports. Believe it or not, some only deal with a handful of flights per day and have perhaps four departure gates maximum. Look on flightradar24.com to see departure lists for any airport to help gauge how busy it is likely to be, especially for the day of week and time you will be flying. The fewer the flights, the later you can risk leaving it.

On arrival at the airport terminal building, follow signs for 'Security'. Have your boarding pass ready, either on your phone or printed off, as you will need to scan the QR code at the barrier gates to proceed to the security queue. As you approach the scanning machines, empty out your water bottle at one of the marked points and remove your wallet, phone and other electrical items and place them in one of the trays provided, along with the clear plastic bag containing liquids if applicable. Coats also need to be removed and placed in trays as do bags. Have your passport ready to be checked.

Once you have retrieved your belongings you are free to peruse the shops on the other side. Take the chance to refill your water bottle or purchase one. Consider buying food or snacks to take on board the plane.

Keep checking the screens for the gate number to appear next to your flight number. When it does, make your way towards your gate. Major airports have dozens of departure gates and require up to 15 minutes on foot as well as a shuttle ride to reach the furthest gates - so do leave sufficient time.

Once you reach your gate you can relax and wait to be called for boarding. Have your boarding pass and passport to hand for a final check.

**Options for travel to your departure airport**

**Driving and parking**

Although driving your own car to the airport and having it ready and waiting to jump into and drive home at the end of your break is a convenient option, official airport car parks charge exorbitant fees these days. If this is your preferred option, it is worth obtaining an online quote to be able to compare the cost of parking your car to other transportation options. Some companies such as Holiday Extras claim to offer discounted airport parking rates; do check to see how their prices compare to booking direct rather than taking their own word for it though. The rule of thumb for official airport car parking is that the further in advance you can book it, the lower the price will be.

Airport hotels sometimes offer competitively priced parking and can on occasion be almost as close as the official airport car parks so are worth exploring.

Surprisingly, the best prices for these can often be found on apps such as 'Justpark' and 'YourParkingSpace' rather than directly with the hotels.

Do think carefully about whether you will feel up to driving home when arriving back at your home airport late in the evening after a long and action-packed day. Driving when overtired can be dangerous, especially if the drive is a long one. If this is likely to adversely affect you then consider a different means of reaching the airport or maybe add a stayover to your trip to facilitate a return flight at a more convenient time of the day so that you will feel fresher after a full night's sleep.

**Drop off and collection by a friend or family member**

Maybe you are in the lucky position of having a kind and helpful family member or close friend willing to drop off and collect you from the airport. Do bear in mind though that the nature of day trips abroad means that you would probably need lifts at (what most would consider) unsociable times of the day and night so it could be too big an ask. Maybe less so if two separate drivers were willing to drive one way each, though.

**Public transport**

National Express runs airport coach transfers to and from many UK airports and the surrounding towns and cities. They often continue running through the night. Megabus is another similar operator. Coach transfers can be excellent value especially if you manage to bag tickets on their special price promotions.

Train services often run between airports and nearby cities. Search online to see if this is the case for your location.

**Airport taxis**

Despite taxis sounding an extremely expensive choice, the fares can work out good value when split between several travellers. Many taxi firms can offer larger vehicles seating up to seven passengers (and for a day trip or one night stay no extra space need to be wasted in the vehicle for luggage) so could prove to be ideal for groups of friends or family travelling together.

A taxi could also be the most practical way of completing the very first and last leg of your journey if travelling by bus or train, should you live some distance from the local railway or bus station or feel unsafe walking home in the dark.

**Enjoy the journey**

It is an inescapable fact that on an EDT travel time makes up a significant part of the day. Rather than viewing the journey as a means to an end, ponder how to make it more enjoyable. Should you be seated with travel companions then travel time can be great for quality catching up time with friends.

Funnily enough, some of the most fascinating individuals I have had the good fortune to meet have been on journeys. Despite having remained in contact with very few of them, when I have struck up conversations with strangers each has had their own story that they were willing to share. Every chance encounter has prompted a little self-reflection and a beneficial reminder that life is short and for the living.

If conversation is not an option, take a paperback book to lose yourself in to pass the time. A mini notebook and pen may also be worth bringing as even a brief change of scene can spark seeds of ideas for changes that we wish to make in our lives. If not recorded immediately, they tend to be forgotten about.

**Coping with tiredness**

The prospect of being able to travel between two countries which happen to be hundreds of miles apart in a single day is a wondrous and exciting one, is it not? However, the flip side is that for it to be feasible to experience enough of what the destination has to offer the day will inevitably be a long one. For those who identify as 'morning larks', jumping out of bed at 4.00am to greet the day could be a doddle. Yet those larks will almost certainly be flagging by early evening, just as those of us who class ourselves as 'night owls' reach our energy peak!

Naturally, you want to be able to enjoy your day as much as possible without feeling fatigued so here are a few tips:

- Rest during 'dead time' such as when you have passed through security at the airport and are sitting in the departure lounge or on the plane. Set an alarm on your phone approximately 45 minutes pre-departure to avoid missing gate calls!
- Even if you are unable to fall asleep, just the action of closing your eyes can have a restorative effect and boost energy levels.
- Drink plenty of water and soft drinks but avoid alcohol.
- Dipping a fingertip in clean cold water and dabbing it across your eyelids can have a reviving effect. Likewise, allow cool water from the tap to flow over the insides of your wrists.
- Avoid getting too hot: being in an overly warm or stuffy environment can instantly have your eyelids drooping. Mini battery-powered fans directed at the face can be effective at counteracting this. Remove unnecessary layers of clothing.

- Consider overnight travel options where available such as the coach service from London 'Victoria' station to Paris 'Bercy Seine' station by Flixbus. The 8 hours on board should permit plenty of rest time and leave you feeling refreshed enough to enjoy spending a full day taking in the sights of Paris before catching the overnight return coach.

**Is extreme travel doable with children?**

It is easy to assume that children cannot cope with long day trips: an impossibility, surely? However, I disagree that need be the case and have undertaken successful trips with my own young offspring. Children are naturally full of curiosity and enthusiasm therefore make excellent travel companions. Though banal for many adults, the prospect of exploring an airport and boarding a plane can be a thrilling one for kids. They often express delight in having their senses bombarded abroad: by an incomprehensible language being spoken all around them, exotic aromas wafting through the air and being mesmerised by unfamiliar street life playing out in front of their eyes. This excitement tends to rub off on older travel companions as it re-awakens our own ability to observe and appreciate the smaller details of life through their eyes. Furthermore, young children are naturally early risers and are happy to be woken earlier than normal to embark on a day trip (a silver-lining parent win). Do not underestimate how privileged they will feel to be permitted to stay up way past their usual bedtime hour either.

From my own experience of travelling with three youngsters, the key thing to bring to guarantee a harmonious trip is plenty of snacks to quash hunger-based grumpiness. A familiar small soft toy or blanket can be useful for encouraging little ones to settle down on planes and trains.

If children become restless then providing them with a focus often helps. Travel activities and diaries tailored to the specific destination are useful. The i-Spy series of pocket-sized books published by Collins Michelin have some apt titles such as 'At the Airport' and 'On a Train Journey' have proved to be godsends in the past. Even impromptu challenges such as to be the first to spot specific things (e.g. a person wearing a red coat, a sign for the toilet or a vending machine) can distract them. Children love the company of other children so seating yourself near another family and making conversation with them and introducing your child to theirs can be worthwhile. I have long been amazed by the ability of children to form instant friendships, unhindered even by language barriers.

**Local navigation of your chosen destination**

**Map Apps**

The days of lugging around bulky folding maps to navigate unfamiliar cities have thankfully passed. The only maps you will need can be found in the compact form of the map app on your smartphone (both Apple and Google maps are excellent). No printed map can stay as updated as digital maps and in addition to searching for specific landmarks or attractions they have invaluable features such as a search function for where you want to get to from your current location (e.g. a specific railway station near the airport you have just landed in). Should you be a complete novice, a quick internet search for 'beginners guide to Apple maps' or 'Google maps' to grasp the basics would be worthwhile.

The search results of any given destination will present all your travel options. You can select from the blue 'drive' option if you were to hire a taxi, or the bus and train options complete with the relevant bus number to look out for as well as the time it would take to walk there.

I would recommend that you have a play around with whichever map app you choose to familiarise yourself with this feature. For example, I have just opened my map app and clicked on the coloured dot icon that demarks my local hospital. Instantly, directions are loaded up and using the drop down box I switched from 'drive' mode of transport to 'public transport'. The instructions displayed on the screen clearly show that this journey would involve a 5 minute walk to the bus stop where I need to catch the number 6 bus, followed by a 4 minute walk after alighting the bus. On pressing the green 'go' link the walking directions for the first step of the journey appear, which guide me to the nearest bus stop. For further guidance, even the bus stand number at the hospital and name of the closest bus stop are detailed.

Information is displayed in real time, meaning that journey times are accurately represented according to traffic flow rates etc. If you were to type in a well-known tourist attraction for example 'Eiffel Tower' right now and scroll down past the directions you will see additional related information including opening times, a 'good to know' section such as accessibility features for wheelchair users, whether credit card payments are accepted, a Wikipedia link for detailed information and the attraction's own website link.

Now, the huge scope that phone map apps hold for planning the minutiae details of your trip is clear and you will be able to appreciate how this digital information source is unbeatable for accuracy. My intention is that you will flick through the listed destinations in the 'Destination Guides' that feature in Part Two of this book to see which of the listed attractions in the city take your fancy, then carry out further research yourself, maybe using your map app as the starting point before you set off for your EDT.

**Downloading maps to use offline**

As internet coverage can be slow and unreliable in places and mobile data is expensive, it is prudent to save an area from your maps app to your phone to then use offline. To do this on Google maps, follow these steps:

- Open the Google Maps app.
- Tap your profile picture or initial then Offline maps.
- Tap Select your own map.
- Adjust the map according to the area you want to download.
- Tap Download.

After downloading an area, use the Google Maps app as you would usually. The downloaded map will guide you to your destination as long as the whole route is within the offline map. However, note that public transport, cycling and walking directions are unavailable offline.

## Asking locals for help with directions

Should you find yourself lost or ever struggle to locate a landmark, do not hesitate to approach a member of the public. Your own sense of judgement is usually reliable when selecting someone to ask. Staff in shops and cafes (if not too busy) are often a good shout. English is the most spoken second language in most countries and Europeans often love an opportunity to practise speaking English with a native. Even if a local does not speak it, don't give up too quickly. Try persevering to explain yourself with the help of a translation app such as Google Translate or pointing at your destination on a map. It is basic human nature to want to help others where we can, and a lot can be conveyed through hand gestures and facial expressions (plus a smile goes a long way). For each positive interaction you have with a local, the more enriched and memorable your experience of the place will be.

Free local maps and tourist guides are often readily available from tour guide company reps as well as airports and railway stations. These are worth grabbing to skim read while you transit to the city centre.

**If things go wrong**

Thousands of individuals traverse Europe daily without a hitch. However, although your chances of joining them are excellent it would be naïve to believe that nothing could ever go wrong, so read on to find out how to reduce the chances of problems occurring and what to do should the worst happen.

**Personal security and scams**

The crime rate in most UK cities is probably comparable to similar sized cities in continental Europe. At the time of writing, the cities that receive the highest number of petty crimes based on anecdotal tourist reports include Barcelona, Paris and Rome.

Being a tourist, or to be more specific, taking on the visible appearance of a tourist, does unfortunately increase the odds of being targeted by petty criminals. Aim to walk purposefully and remain aware of your surroundings. Avoid making direct eye contact with strangers and being drawn into conversations with them. Distracting you with conversation or a 'dropped' item is a common trick to enable a criminal's accomplice to grab your bag or slip a wallet from a pocket. Naturally, you will want to take a few photos during the day but when you stop to do so have a quick scan around to monitor who else is around. Leave flashy diamond jewellery and expensive designer bags at home and consider a cross-body bag or backpack rather than a less secure clutch bag that could be easily grabbed by an opportunist thief looking for easy pickings.

For transporting your bank cards and cash a money belt is the best option, tucked out of view under your waistband. Experienced travellers also recommend that you email yourself a copy of your main passport page, credit card and insurance documents including relevant emergency telephone numbers.

Being clued up on current scams prevalent in some of the larger cities is beneficial. Do not be put off visiting them but being forewarned is forearmed and you can relax and enjoy yourself more knowing that you are clued up. As the prevalent scams tend to change over time, carry out an internet search with the name of your destination city plus the keywords 'tourist scams'.

Should you find yourself the victim of a theft or other crime, find the nearest police station via the Maps app. When reporting the crime, request a 'crime reference number' which is needed to make a claim on your travel insurance.

**Medical attention**

The telephone numbers of the relevant emergency (ambulance) service for any destination country can be quickly found by an internet search.

Should an emergency ambulance not be necessary then call a local taxi to transport you to the closest hospital.
See the earlier section on travel insurance, in particular the importance of applying for and carrying an EHIC or GHIC card in addition to standard travel insurance.

**Delayed or cancelled flights home**

In the unlikely scenario of your return travel plans being thwarted, it can be prudent to spend a few minutes online to research a backup plan for returning home, especially if it is crucial that you be home by the next day. This could include checking out alternative airports and relevant flights that depart from it (which could even be in bordering countries) and a means of reaching the airport.

Allow plenty of time to get back to the airport/Eurostar station for the return journey as unexpected delays can arise. It is important to bear in mind that commuter rush hours occur in foreign cities just as they do here, with the associated packed trains and buses. Enough spare money to book an Uber or taxi could mean the difference in making it to airport in time for the flight home or not. Being aware of an alternative route home e.g. on a Eurostar train or flying from another nearby airport that has flights later that same day can be reassuring.

Some day trippers elect to tuck away clean underwear in their bag just in case, plus an extra day's medication (if applicable). Other essentials could include painkillers, a toothbrush and mini travel toothpaste tube and a phone charger. While it may feel annoying to carry them around and have no need to use them, should you be delayed you would no doubt be relieved and pleased at your foresight.

Frustrating as delays can be, try to stay calm and do not allow the inconvenience to detract from the enjoyment experienced earlier in the day. These things happen and if you have either a good book to get absorbed by or an amiable travel companion to chat to, the time will pass faster than it would if you succumbed to negative feelings and resentment. You have no control over such happenings and experiences that do not go to plan are all part of the rich tapestry of life.

# Part Two: Destination Guides

## Destination Guides

Whet your travel appetite by poring over the following guides to a selection of over 50 of the most popular destinations that low-cost airlines fly to in Europe, all within approximately three and a half hours flight time from England. Most of the capital cities are covered, as well as some lesser known but equally rewarding places. It goes without saying that many more countries and cities could have been included and countless others are well worth visiting. I strongly encourage you to cast your net as wide as possible to explore the full range of destinations on offer from your closest airport that only the requirement to keep this book to a comfortable size to hold forced me to exclude.

Each guide aims to cater to the interests of a wide range of travellers so there should be something to interest everyone, from history buffs to sports fans. A selection of places of interest are listed for you to 'pick and mix' the ones that most appeal to your tastes. Many visitor attractions close at least one day of the week so please do check the most up-to-date source (usually the official website) for opening days and times to avoid disappointment.

At the end of each destination guide is the all-important section advising how you can reach the city centre from the airport or Eurostar train station with details on where to purchase tickets. Fortunately, most modern ticket machines abroad tend to have an

English-language option (as well as additional languages) and accept payment by credit or debit card.

Many destinations have more places of interest than can realistically be visited in a single day, which provides the perfect excuse to plan a return visit in the future. Even after feeling you have seen all you desire to see in a first visit to a destination, it could prove worthwhile to carry out a little extra research for additional gems of places within an hour or so by train that are worthy of a visit in themselves. I have included some but there will no doubt be myriad others.

For destinations that are not covered within this book, a useful starting point to research potential places of interest is the city's tourist information organisation. Simply searching online for 'visit X', substituting X with your destination name, should yield fruitful results. Tripadvisor.com website also lists highly rated attractions for each destination. Atlasobscura.com is a terrific site to discover quirky, hidden gems of places to try in any destination.

Given that the primary focus is on day trips abroad, detailed information on accommodation falls outside the scope of this book. However, there are countless websites dedicated to providing accommodation options covering every corner of Europe. Should you decide to turn your day trip into an overnighter, it is best to use well-known platforms to book if needed and opt for accommodation providers with consistently high ratings, positive reviews and which offer free cancellation. Always check the location of each accommodation carefully as the more central the better to maximise the time on a short overnight trip.

The destinations have been grouped into European geographical regions and then into countries for simplicity's sake.

# Northern Europe

## England

### London

A vast city, London is packed to the rafters with iconic landmarks, royal history and traditions and world class museums. As the saying goes, 'he who is tired of London is tired of life', so there is no excuse to feel bored in this massive metropolis.

**A few suggestions on how to spend a day in London:**

Most of the places of interest listed below are in relatively close proximity, for ease of packing more into a short space of time. Clustered around the **river Thames**, they also involve a lot of walking alongside and crisscrossing her varied bridges for added enjoyment. As you stroll, keep an eye out for **Shakespeare's Globe theatre** just off the South Bank- a building with distinctive white round walls and striking timber beam detailing. After dark, enjoy a feast for the eyes in the form of **the Illuminated River Project** along **South Bank**'s riverside. An orchestrated series of lights span nine bridges.
- **Sky Garden** is a three-storey glass dome atop a skyscraper that provides far-reaching views of the city. The landscaped gardens offer an oasis

of calm in the heart of the city, with observation decks and an open-air terrace. Restaurants are available but must be booked in advance, or the Sky Pod Bar serves drinks. Simply reserve a free time slot in advance on their website to be able to enter the Sky Garden.
- **Tower Bridge** is a magnificent and imposing structure spanning the river Thames. Take a few panoramic photos and cross it on foot to reach the Tower of London.
- **The Tower of London** is an unmissable sight positioned right in front of Tower Bridge. This castle with over 1,000 years of history is home to the Crown Jewels. Be sure to book a tour with one of the knowledgeable and entertaining Beefeater Warders.
- Located a little further along the river Thames, the **London Eye observation wheel** offers unobstructed views from its glass pods. Enjoy spotting well-known buildings such as Buckingham Palace, Big Ben, and The Shard during the 30-minute ride.
- **Leake Street,** beneath the tracks of Waterloo station, is a 300 metre long graffiti tunnel where you can meet local street artists, muse at the murals and even add to them. Hang out at one of the quirky bars.
- The **Tate Modern** art gallery displays an eclectic range of paintings, sculptures and large-scale installations from artists around the

world including Pablo Picasso and Henri Matisse.

- **Big Ben clock tower and the Houses of Parliament** form an impressive sight, best viewed from **Westminster Bridge**. The buildings are amongst the most recognisable in the world. Each one of Big Ben's clock faces measures nearly seven metres wide.
- **Westminster Abbey** is another iconic London building, the venue of choice for many British royal weddings. It has been the coronation church since 1066. Visitors can enjoy viewing a range of paintings, stained glass, textiles and books plus the largest collection of monumental sculptures of the UK.
- **Covent Garden** includes a covered market selling a range of eclectic gifts as well as restaurants, bars, and boutiques. Street performers with varied acts provide a steady stream of entertainment.
- **Buckingham Palace** is renowned worldwide as a longtime royal home. The balcony has seen many monarchs make an appearance in front of huge crowds. Don't miss the changing of the guard: the current schedules are every Monday, Wednesday, Friday and Sunday at 11.00 each morning at Buckingham Palace. Prior to the ceremony at Buckingham Palace, you can also stroll over to the nearby **Wellington Barracks** at 10.30 as the guards prepare to

leave for Buckingham Palace (crowds tend to be smaller here).

The three museums below are all on Exhibition Road in South Kensington so art and culture lovers would have plenty to keep them occupied. All are free to enter:

- The **Victoria and Albert Museum (V & A)**, in Kensington contains arguably the largest collection of art and design displays in the world, spanning five thousand years. The museum building itself is stunningly impressive with features of classic Victorian architecture.
- The **Natural History Museum** is not far from the V & A and houses a massive range of specimens (many of significant size, including dinosaur skeletons). It is worth a visit for the architecture alone, as it is recognised as one of the most celebrated Gothic revival buildings nationally, intended to be a 'cathedral to nature' by its architect.
- The **Science Museum** claims to be 'the home of human ingenuity' with award-winning exhibitions and iconic objects to marvel at. Plenty of interactive and hands-on exhibits are available to interest younger visitors too.

**A day out a little further afield:**

**Kew Gardens** is a must for nature and plant lovers. It boasts the largest and most diverse botanical collection in the world. Set in the site of a former royal estate you can enjoy beautifully landscaped displays. The highlight is climbing up to and along the Treetop Walkway, sited 18 metres above ground to provide a spectacular viewing point of the tree canopy ecosystems, with many types of birds and insects to spot.

**How to reach London city from the airport:**

Three main airports serve London but the two most frequently used by low-cost European carriers are Stansted and Gatwick.

From Stansted follow signs to the Stansted Express train. This departs every 15 minutes during the day and takes 48 minutes to reach central London. Pre book tickets on the Stansted Express website or buy from ticket machines at stations.

From Gatwick, the Gatwick Express train departs every 15 minutes and takes only 30 minutes to reach central London. Pre book tickets on the Gatwick Express website or buy from ticket machines at stations.

## Scotland

## Edinburgh

Steeped in history, Scotland's capital Edinburgh is well-known for its medieval old town, stunning viewpoints, world-class art, and charming whisky pubs. Wish to see familiar Harry Potter sites and explore a 12th-century castle that sits atop an extinct volcano? Look no further.

**A few suggestions on how to spend a day in Edinburgh:**

- Nature lovers can visit the **Royal Botanical Garden**, an urban jungle with giant lily pads and gorgeous flowers and plants.
- For panoramic views of the city, climb **Arthur's Seat**. The climb to the top of this ancient volcano takes about 45 minutes.
- Art lovers will want to spend a few hours at the **Scottish National Gallery of Modern Art** which is situated inside two grand Georgian mansions.
- Home to the oldest crown jewels in the UK, **Edinburgh Castle** is the most popular tourist

attraction in the city. Hear the firing of the One o'Clock Gun, go on a guided tour with a castle steward, and try homemade scones with strawberry jam at the traditional tea room.
- Walk down the **Royal Mile**, a succession of streets that run from the castle to the **Holyrood Palace**. These busy streets are dotted with souvenir shops, traditional restaurants and museums.
- Shopaholics visiting Edinburgh can check out the winding **Victoria Street** and admire the beautiful Flemish-style buildings. This elegantly curved street is lined with an eclectic mix of boutiques, galleries, and speciality shops.
- Whisky lovers can visit the Scotch Whisky Experience and go on a tour of the virtual distillery. This place features the largest collection of whisky bottles in the world.
- See **Harry Potter sites** such as Nicolson's Café, the Elephant House, and Greyfriars Kirkyard.
- Located just a short walk from the city centre, **Dean Village** is a picturesque neighbourhood known for its medieval streets lined with historic buildings. Snap a photo in front of the Well Court, a red sandstone house with a clock tower.

**Traditional foods to try in Edinburgh:**

**Haggis** – made of sheep heart, liver, and lungs and served with mashed turnips and potatoes in the form of a pudding. Locals swear it tastes delicious!

**Fish Supper**- juicy fried fish in a crispy batter served with fresh chips.

## How to reach the city from the airport:

Edinburgh Airport is the main airport. The easiest way to reach the centre from the airport is by hopping on a tram. Trams depart every seven minutes between 07:00 and 19:00. Early in the morning and late in the evening, trams depart every 10 minutes. The last tram departs at 22:48.

The airport tram stop is just outside the main terminal. The journey via tram from the airport to the city centre takes 35 minutes. You can buy tram tickets online or from the ticket vending machines at the airport.

## How to reach Edinburgh from London on the Caledonian Sleeper train:

The Caledonian Sleeper departs from London Euston station every night of the week apart from Saturdays at 23:45 (23:30 Sundays). You will reach Edinburgh's Waverley station in about 7 hours and 30 minutes. Though not a budget option, the beds on board offer a reasonable level of comfort and travelling by night leaves a full day free for exploring the many delights that Edinburgh can offer.

Booking a fortnight or more in advance tends to secure the best value fares.

# Wales

## Cardiff

Home to global sports events, a stunning waterfront complex and modern and innovative facilities, Cardiff oozes charm. The capital of Wales offers something for everyone.

**A few suggestions on how to spend a day in Cardiff:**

- **Mermaid Quay** is a large waterfront complex in Cardiff Bay. Visitors can take a ride on the Ferris wheel, watch stand-up comedy performances at the Glee Club and visit a fabulous science centre called **Techniquest** housing over 100 interactive exhibits relating to space.
- Sports fans can check out the magnificent **Principality Stadium**. This 74,500-seater stadium has hosted events like the Rugby World Cup and the UEFA Champions League finals. Ed Sheeran and the Rolling Stones have performed here amongst many other stars.

- History buffs and culture vultures visiting Cardiff will want to see the extraordinary **Cardiff Castle**. The tour of the castle is about 50 minutes long and allows visitors to see everything from floral carvings to gold and marble furnishings.
- Nature lovers can look forward to visiting the lovely **Bute Park**. Attached to Cardiff Castle, this beautiful park is home to picturesque gardens with unique trees and flowers, winding paths, sculptures and much more.
- Art lovers will be delighted to hear that **National Museum Cardiff** is home to one of the finest Impressionist art collections in Europe. In addition to amazing paintings, the museum also includes a range of ceramics, drawings and sculptures.
- Cardiff is a great place to go on a shopping spree and enjoy extraordinary architecture at the same time. There are seven quaint **Victorian & Edwardian shopping arcades** dating back to the 19th century in the city centre.
- Established back in 1894, **Spillers Records** claims to be the world's oldest record shop. You will find this small shop with cool vinyl offerings in the **Morgan Arcade**. It is a must-visit place for music fans staying in Cardiff.
- Seeing the city from the water is a unique experience. Hop on a **boat tour** either at Cardiff Bay or Cardiff City Centre in Bute Park

and experience the Welsh capital from a different perspective.
- Travellers short on time can get on one of the classic double-decker buses and join a hop-on-hop-off tour. Included in a 24-hour ticket is an informative audio commentary.

**How to reach Cardiff city centre from the airport:**

The national airport for Wales is Cardiff Airport. The best way to get from Cardiff Airport to the city centre is with the T9 Cardiff Airport Express Bus. The bus runs every 20-30 minutes and bus travel time is 40 minutes. Purchase your ticket from the bus driver or at the ticket counter at the airport.

# Northern Ireland

## Belfast

Capital of Northern Ireland and birthplace of the Titanic, Belfast is famed for its industrial and maritime heritage.

Northern Ireland's capital also has a brilliant pub scene and spectacular scientific exhibitions. Venture outside the city gates to find stunning countryside areas and awe-inspiring natural wonders.

**A few suggestions on how to spend a day in Belfast:**

- **Titanic Belfast** is the number one tourist attraction. This monumental museum is dedicated to the most famous ship in the world: the legendary Titanic. Thanks to multisensory technology, visitors will be sent back to the 1910s when the Titanic and her sister ships were constructed. The self-guided Titanic Experience tour includes a visit to nine interpretive and interactive galleries.
- Foodies should check out the lively **St George's Market** on the weekends. From

antiques and furniture to delicious seafood, colourful sweets and free jazz music performances, this place has it all.
- For spectacular city views, visit the **Victoria Square shopping centre** where you will find the iconic dome. Rising high above the city's skyline, this glittering glass dome offers magnificent views across Belfast.
- Your next stop is the **Botanic Gardens**. Once a private park, this colourful place is home to a variety of plants and trees. The most interesting attraction here is the Palm House, the world's first curvilinear glasshouse which is home to the 11-metre-high globe spear lily. Visit the indoor sunken tropical ravine garden to spot orchid plants and bananas.
- **Cave Hill Country Park** is where you will find Belfast Castle. Snap a photo in front of this 19th–century Baronial-style castle and see the interior which includes playrooms, bedrooms, kitchens and a gigantic dining room.
- Science freaks and travellers visiting Belfast with kids will want to pay a visit to **W5**, an interactive museum which houses over 250 hands-on stations spread across four exhibition zones.

**A few recommendations on day trips from Belfast:**

- Visit the beautiful **Giant's Causeway**, a UNESCO World Heritage site which is home to a series of geometric basalt columns. Take the train to Coleraine from Belfast's Great Victoria Street in about 1 hour 15 minutes. From there, take the 170 or 420 bus which run directly to the Causeway.
- One of the most photographed spots in the region, **Carrick-A-Rede Bridge** is a dramatic suspension bridge located just west of Giant's Causeway.
- Game of Thrones fans will want to visit **Dark Hedges**, a famous filming location for the popular TV show. This dark street is lined with beech trees and looks stunning. This is apparently the most photographed spot in the whole of Northern Ireland.

**How to reach Belfast city from the airport:**

You will land at Belfast Airport. The best way to reach the city centre is with the Airport Express 300 Service bus which runs from the terminal building every 15 to 20 minutes. You can purchase tickets from the information desk in the Arrivals area, from the ticket machines in the bus shelter area, or from the driver.

Travel time is 30 to 45 minutes depending on the traffic.

# Republic of Ireland

## Dublin

Ireland's capital, Dublin, is a city of cool art venues, beautiful Georgian architecture and lively pubs serving Guinness beer. The city is relatively compact and easy to get around, making it an ideal destination for a express day trip.

### A few suggestions on how to spend a day in Dublin:

- **The Guinness Storehouse** is the top tourist attraction in Dublin, so it is advisable to purchase your ticket before the trip. Join a guided tour through seven floors dedicated to Irish Brewing and the Guinness family. The tour ends at the Gravity Bar on the seventh floor where you can enjoy a fresh pint of Guinness. The views of the Dublin skyline from the bar are amazing.
- A busy riverside area with cobbled streets, **Temple Bar** is buzzing with restaurants, pubs and live music. It is an ideal place to sample Irish cuisine, drink beer and listen to live folk

music. Drink prices are high, but the atmosphere and ambiance are unrivalled.
- To experience Dublin from a unique perspective, hop on a **river cruise** on the River Liffey.
- Whiskey lovers can go on a tour of the **Old Jameson Distillery**.
- In the afternoon, visit historic **Dublin Castle** which was built on the site of a former Viking settlement. You can go for a stroll in the **Dubh Linn gardens** or join one of the self-guided and guided tours of the castle.
- Sports fans visiting Dublin can stop by the legendary **Croke Park Stadium**. Also known as Croker, the stadium is an institution for Irish sports fans. To learn more about the Gaelic Athletic Association and to test your own sporting skills, visit the on-site **GAA museum**.

**Traditional foods to try:**

**Boxty Pancakes** are traditional Irish potato pancakes eaten with butter or sugar.
**Barmbrack** is richly fruited bread topped with butter.

**How to reach Dublin city from the airport:**

The Dublin Express bus is the easiest option for getting from the airport to the city centre. The bus stops directly outside of terminals 1 and 2.

Travellers can book their bus tickets online in advance, at terminal bus stops, and directly from the driver with a bank card. These buses leave the terminals every 15 minutes and the journey to the city centre is approximately 30 minutes long depending on traffic.

## Cork

The second-largest city in the Republic of Ireland, Cork is famed for its lively pubs, vibrant art galleries and artisan coffee shops. It has a large student population and is home to one of the world's largest natural harbours.

**A few suggestions on how to spend a day in Cork:**

- Serving Cork City since 1788, the **English Market** is a great place to kick off your travel itinerary. This impressive food market is filled with fresh local produce. From locally made buffalo mozzarella and gourmet sausages to artisan cakes, the English Market has it all. Try the local salty slice of beef which is steamed in stout beer.

- Let your curiosity lead you to **Cork City Gaol**, a former prison transformed into a museum. Learn about 19th and early 20th-century prison life in Cork and sneak a peek at authentically furnished cells and corridors.
- No visit to the city is complete without stopping by the 17th-century **Church of St. Anne**. For spectacular views of Cork, climb the 170-foot-high **Shandon Bell Tower**.
- **Fitzgerald Park** is a great spot to spend an afternoon in Cork. Located a stone's throw from University College Cork, the park is home to wandering paths, sculptures and colourful flower beds.
- Cork city used to be the centre of Europe's butter trade. Therefore, it comes as no surprise that the **Cork Butter Museum** is one of the best tourist attractions here. Learn more about domestic butter-making at this unusual museum.
- Art lovers should not miss the **Crawford Municipal Art Gallery** which houses a vast collection of Irish art including sculptures, paintings and installations.
- Venture outside the city gates and visit **Blarney Castle**. Here, you will find the world famous Blarney Stone, picturesque gardens and Witch's Kitchen which was home to the first Irish cave dwellers.

**How to get from the airport to the city centre:**

Cork Airport (ORK) is served by a scheduled bus service. Take the 225 or 226 bus line to Cork city centre and Parnell Place Bus Station. These routes operate every 30 minutes on weekdays and every 60 minutes on Sundays.

You can purchase tickets on the bus or from the ticket machines located at the bus stop which is located right in from of the terminal building. It will take you about 20 minutes to reach the city centre.

## Denmark

### Copenhagen

The buzzing capital of Denmark, Copenhagen is one of the most charming cities in Northern Europe. Known for its photogenic waterfront, elegant palaces and cutting-edge restaurants this vibrant city located on the islands of Zealand and Amager is packed with tourist attractions.

**A few suggestions on how to spend a day in Copenhagen:**

- With its lush gardens, floral displays, stunning architecture, illuminated fountains and open-air theatres, **Tivoli Gardens** is the number one tourist attraction in the city. The themes change every season and the decorations are always a sight to behold. Many different rides and activities are available at the park, with an option for everyone. Be aware that Tivoli is mostly closed over the winter months.

- Soak up the sights at **Nyhavn**, an historic waterfront area fringed by brightly painted townhouses, old wooden ships and fabulous seafood dining establishments. Bustling with tourists and locals, it is the most photographed area of the city.
- Foodies spending a day or two in Copenhagen will want to check out the two glass-and-steel market halls at **Torvehallerne**. There are more than 80 vendors selling everything from fresh produce and spices to delicious seafood and meats at Torvehallerne. Visit small restaurants and take-away eateries to try artisan Danish cheeses, the duck confit sandwich, gourmet chocolate and much more.
- You will find the **Little Mermaid statue** right next to the **Langelinie promenade**. Created as a tribute to the world-famous author Hans Christian Andersen, this beautiful state is one of the most famous landmarks in Copenhagen.
- Shopaholics can visit **Strøget**, a pedestrian street lined with designer brands and hip boutiques. If you prefer independent local shops, visit the narrow side streets.
- There is no shortage of magnificent museums in Copenhagen. Home to an extensive

collection of Danish and European works, **Statens Museum for Kunst** (Denmark's national art museum) is situated inside a beautiful modern building. To see pieces by Picasso and Giacometti, visit the **Louisiana Museum of Modern Art.**
- Nature lovers will want to go to **the Copenhagen Botanical Garden**. Some of the highlights include a historic Victorian greenhouse, a rhododendron garden and a butterfly house.

**Getting to the city centre from the airport:**

The main international gateway to Denmark is Copenhagen Airport, locally known as Kastrup Airport. Take the M2 metro line from the airport to reach central locations in the city centre such as Kongens Nytorv and Nørreport.

Trains depart every 2 minutes and the journey to the city centre takes approximately 15 minutes. The airport metro station is located right next to the arrivals hall. Purchase metro tickets from the ticket machines in the arrivals area or from the DSB ticket sales booth.

## Billund

Are you a fan of Lego? If so, Denmark's beloved theme park town promises to keep you entertained for a day or so. Welcome to Billund, the birthplace of LEGO. This is an ideal destination to visit with the little ones. Billund is a tiny town with just 7,000 residents, of which two-thirds are employed at the Lego toy company. There are three main tourist attractions in Billund: Legoland, the Lego House and Lalandia.

**A few suggestions on how to spend a day in Billund:**

- In terms of the number of visitors, **Legoland** is the biggest tourist attraction in Denmark.

This fabulous amusement park contains nine LEGO-themed lands, splash rides, coasters and 4D cinemas. You will also have a chance to see world-known monuments such as the Acropolis and the Statue of Liberty built with thousands of Lego bricks. Some of the most popular rides at Legoland include Emmett's Flying Adventure Masters of Flight, NINJAGO the Ride and Apocalypseburg Sky Battle.

- The **Lego House** hosts an interactive centre, toy shop and Lego art gallery. Whether you wish to create a Lego face, make your own Lego racing car, or just chill by the Lego waterfall, there is so much to do and see at this interactive playground. Lego fans will also want to visit the Mini Chef where they are served by robots and can build their own meals.
- Scandinavia's biggest amusement and activity complex, **Lalandia** will keep you and your kids entertained for a few hours. From bowling alleys and climbing walls to a huge indoor waterpark with high-speed slides, this activity complex in Billund has it all. While the kids play crazy golf and other supervised games, adults can visit the wellness area which offers everything from spa treatments and saunas to massages.

**A couple of recommendations on day trips from Billund:**

- Hop on a bus to the nearby town of **Vejle** to admire picturesque old townhouses.
- Wish to go on an African safari in Denmark? Pay a visit to **Givskud Zoo** and hop on a safari bus to spot giraffes, lemurs and zebras.

## How to reach Billund town centre from the airport:

The centre of the city is located just a few miles from Billund Airport. The best way to reach the city centre is via the 43 bus route. Buses run a few times an hour and take around 10 minutes to reach the centre.
Purchase your bus tickets online, from the bus driver, or the ticket machine in the arrivals hall. The bus stop is located right in front of the airport building.

### Sweden

### Stockholm

With impressive architecture, cobbled streets, stunning museums and innovative dining, Stockholm is one of the coolest Scandinavian cities to visit. Spread across 14 islands, Sweden's elegant capital is home to one of the best-preserved medieval centres in Europe, dotted with a wide range of tourist attractions.

## A few suggestions on how to spend a day in Stockholm:

- A fairytale district with cobbled streets and colourful buildings, **Gamla Stan** (the 'Old Town') is the beating heart of Stockholm. This enchanting area is packed with eclectic boutiques, delightful cafes and dining establishments.
- Gamla Stan is where you will find one of the largest royal abodes in Europe: the wonderful **Royal Palace**. This 18th-century building is still the official residence of the Swedish royal family. However, you can visit a few of the rooms such as the Royal Apartments and the Museum of Antiquities.
- Discover world-class museums at **Djurgården**, one of the islands in Stockholm. To learn more about Swedish history, drop by the Nordic Museum. There is also the spectacular **ABBA Museum,** dedicated to the most famous band from Sweden. Art lovers visiting Stockholm will want to visit **Fotografiska Museet** and **Moderna Museet**.
- Having lots of islands, Stockholm is a great place to go on a boat cruise. If you are short on time and wish to see some of the main sights from a different perspective, book one of these amazing boat trips.
- **Södermalm**, or just Söder, is one of the most vibrant districts in the city. Here, you will find vintage stores, art galleries, boutiques, and eclectic bars. For magnificent views of

Stockholm, climb the **Skinnarviksberget** which is the highest point in the city.

- Stockholm's extensive **metro** is more than just your ordinary transit system. With superb artworks, mosaics, rock formations and sculptures created by local artists, the metro stations in the capital of Sweden collectively form an artistic paradise.
- The **Östermalm Market Hall** is a great spot to sample tasty traditional Swedish delicacies such as cured fish and Swedish meatballs.
- If you are planning to spend the night in the city, book tickets for a symphony, opera, or ballet performance at the **Royal Swedish Opera**.

**Getting from the airport to the city centre:**

Stockholm-Arlanda Airport is located 25 miles north of the city centre. The Arlanda Express train provides a shuttle service between the airport and the Central Station in Stockholm every 10 to 15 minutes. The platform is easily accessible underneath the arrival terminals and travel time is 18 minutes. Purchase tickets online, at the airport information desks or from a ticket machine.

## Finland

## Helsinki

Helsinki is a city of traditional saunas, art galleries and green spaces. With fewer than one million residents, the capital of Finland is small enough to be explored on foot. If you don't mind cold and snowy weather over the winter months, Helsinki is an excellent destination for a quick day trip or a weekend getaway.

**A few suggestions on how to spend a day in Helsinki:**

- Situated inside an ultra-modern building, **Kiasma** is the most famous art gallery in Finland. Check out an impressive collection of nearly 9,000 artworks created by Finnish artists.
- The **National Museum of Finland** is centred on Finnish history and houses artefacts such as jewellery, coins, tools, weapons and much more.
- To admire the beauty of modern and contemporary art in Helsinki, stop by **Amos Rex**.
- There is also the **Post Museum**, a quirky museum dedicated to the history of the postal service in Finland.
- **Kauppatori** is a bustling market square where you can purchase souvenirs, flowers and sample delicious traditional Finnish foods such as Mustikkapiirakka (Blueberry Pie) and Kaalikääryleet (steamed cabbage leaves with beef).
- No visit to Helsinki is complete without going to a traditional **Finnish sauna**. Beloved by Finns, there are more than 2.5 million saunas in the country.
- In fine weather, go for a stroll in one of the beautiful parks such as **Esplanade Park and Kaivopuisto Park**.

- In the afternoon, visit the **Olympic Stadium (Helsingin Olympiastadion)**. A 72-meter-high tower is served by a lift and offers panoramic views of the city.

**A day trip from Helsinki:**

- Take one of the numerous ferries to **Tallinn** (Estonia) and explore its picturesque **Old Town**. Nature lovers can go on a day trip to **Nuuksio National Park**, one of the finest hiking destinations in the region.

**Getting to the city centre from the airport:**

Helsinki-Vantaa Airport is located 14 miles from the centre of the city. The best way to reach the Helsinki Central Railway Station is to take the "I" or "P" train from the Helsinki Airport's railway station which is located under the terminal. Just take the lift in the arrivals hall.

Trains leave the airport every 10 minutes during peak hours and the journey from the airport to the city centre takes around 30 minutes. Train tickets can be purchased via the HSL mobile app or from the ticket machine at the train platform. Bear in mind that some machines at the airport only accept card payments.

## Norway

## Oslo

From world-class museums featuring inspiring exhibits to spectacular architecture, with the bonus of incredible nature right on the doorstep, the bustling Norwegian capital of Oslo has everything needed for a great getaway.

**A few suggestions on how to spend a day in Oslo:**

- To learn more about the history of the city, pay a visit to the 13th-century medieval **Akershus Fortress**. The guided tour includes a visit to the banquet halls, government reception rooms, dungeons, and a Royal mausoleum.
- Located right on the harbour, the **Oslo Opera House** is an award-winning building known for its stunning architecture. Climb the roof of Scandinavia's most iconic modern building to enjoy magnificent views of the city.
- Check out **Vigeland Sculpture Park**. The world's largest sculpture park featuring works by a single artist is home to 200 bronze, granite and iron statues.
- To discover Oslo's magnificent waterways (fjords), hop on an electric **ferry boat to Oslofjord**. The two-hour long fjord sightseeing cruise allows travellers to see natural attractions such as Hoveøya Island and Bygdøy Peninsula.
- Oslo is a city of museums. Home to three of the most important Viking ships, the **Viking Ship Museum** is a fascinating place to visit. Art lovers will want to check out the **MUNCH Museum** and the **Astrup Fearnley Museum of Modern Art**.
- Sports fans looking for things to do in Oslo can be wowed by **Holmenkollbakken Hill**, the country's most famous ski jump tower. Besides the ramp, there is a cool **Ski Museum**.

- Foodies in Oslo should make a beeline for the **Mathallen Food Hall**. Situated inside a brick industrial building, this hall is home to many food stalls, speciality shops and cafes. Sample contemporary Nordic cuisine and delicacies from all over the world.

**Getting from the airport to the city centre:**

Norway's main international airport, Oslo Lufthavn is located 18 miles from Oslo at Gardermoen. Bear in mind that some budget flights land at Oslo Torp airport which is 75 miles from Oslo and takes the best part of 2 hours to reach Oslo city centre, so it is best avoided.

The best way to reach the city centre from Oslo Lufthavn is via Flytoget's Airport Express trains that depart every 10 minutes. The journey to Oslo Central Station takes 20 minutes. After passing through customs, turn right and you will see Flytoget Airport Express signs. Purchase tickets online, through the Flytoget App, or the ticket machines in the arrivals hall.

## Iceland

### Reykjavik

With a population of only around 130,000 people, Reykjavik is easy to explore on foot. From quirky museums and art galleries in the city centre area to transcendental northern lights safaris and day trips to some breathtaking nature spots, the capital of Iceland offers an abundance of experiences.

**A few suggestions on how to spend a day in Reykjavik**

- **Hallgrimskirkja** is one of the most unique churches in Iceland. With a distinctively curved spire, basalt cliffs and columns, its design is inspired by the Icelandic natural features. Take the lift to the observation platform for impressive views over the city centre.
- Located just around the corner from the church, the **Einar Jónsson Sculpture Park and Museum** is dedicated to one of the most famous sculptors in Iceland. See more than 25 bronze casts created by the symbolist Einar Jónsson.
- Wish to go shopping in Reykjavik? The city has a few good **shopping malls** such as Laugavegur, Kringlan and Smaralind. Laugavegur is located in the city centre, while Smaralind is in Kopavogur.
- Culture vultures visiting Reykjavik can spend a few hours at the **National Museum of Iceland**. With an impressive collection of Icelandic objects and artefacts, it is a great place to learn about the history and culture of Iceland. The National Museum of Iceland is

home to 2,000 artefacts found all over the country.
- Iceland is one of the best places in the world to view the northern lights. Join a **northern lights tour** with a professional guide to see the spectacular natural phenomenon. One of the best places to experience the northern lights is by the seaside at **Seltjarnarnes**. The optimal time to spot the northern lights in Iceland is between October and March.

**Traditional foods to try:**

**Skyr** is a dairy product similar to Greek yoghurt and is eaten with milk and fruit or berries.

**Rúgbrauð** is a traditional dark brown rye bread eaten as a side dish.

**How to get from the airport to the city centre:**

Located 30 kilometres from Reykjavik, Keflavik Airport is the main airport. The best way to get to the city is by the Flybus (private bus company). The bus stop is located outside the arrivals exit and the journey takes between 45 to 90 minutes. Alight at BSI, Reykjavík's main bus terminal. A Flybus is scheduled to depart 35 to 45 minutes after every arrival. Purchase tickets online or at the Flybus stand in the arrivals hall.

<u>**Western Europe**</u>
<u>**France**</u>

## Paris

Paris spoils visitors for choice with exquisite palaces, world-famous museums and historic monuments. It is regarded as one of the most romantic cities in the world. This guide to visiting the City of Light will help you maximise your time.

**A few suggestions on how to spend a day in Paris:**

- The majestic **Eiffel Tower** is the most famous tourist attraction in Paris. If you are short on time, going up the tower is probably not the best idea as much time will be wasted on queuing. Instead, snap a photo in front of the iconic tower or from one of the popular viewpoints **(Quai Branly Museum**, the **Ferris wheel** in the Tuileries Gardens and **Champ-de-Mars)**.
- Art lovers will want to visit the **Louvre**, one of the most popular art museums in the world. Book your tickets in advance to beat the queues.
- Stop by the mighty **Arc de Triomphe**, one of the city's most recognisable landmarks. With impressive sculptures that adorn its pillars, this iconic monument honours those who gave their lives for France during the French Revolution.
- Admire the imposing Gothic structure of **Notre Dame Cathedral.**

- Visit the most famous bookstore in Paris, **Shakespeare & Company**.
- Book a **Seine River boat tour** and enjoy attractions like Musée d'Orsay, the Grand and Petit Palais and the Eiffel Tower from a different perspective.
- Go for a stroll in the picturesque **Luxembourg Gardens**. Locally known as "Luco", this charming park is home to more than 100 statues, chestnut trees, lush flowers, and a greenhouse with an impressive orchid collection.
- With its cobbled streets, hillside houses and cute cafes, **Montmartre** in Paris's northern 18th arrondissement is one of the most charming places to wander. Don't forget to pause by the white-domed **Basilica of Sacre Coeur**.

**How to reach the city from the airport:**

Charles de Gaulle is the main airport in Paris. The best way to reach the city centre from the airport is via train. Keep in mind that the main airport in Paris has two railway stations: Aéroport Charles de Gaulle 1 and Aéroport Charles de Gaulle 2. The trains run approximately every 10-15 minutes and the journey lasts approximately 30 minutes. Purchase your train tickets through the station's ticket machines or from the ticket kiosks.

**How to reach Paris by Eurostar train:**

The Eurostar train travels directly from London St Pancras station to Paris Gare du Nord in just 2 hours and 16 minutes.

**How to reach Paris by Coach from London:**

There is a good value coach service operating from London Victoria station to Paris Bercy Seine station by Flixbus. If selecting the overnight service, the eight hours on board should (in theory) permit plenty of rest time to leave you refreshed and raring to spend a full day taking in the sights of Paris, before catching the overnight return coach. Book tickets at least a week in advance for the best value.

# Nice

The fifth largest city in France is known for its beautiful seafront promenade, charming medieval castles and an abundance of green parks. Venture outside the city to locate quaint villages and medieval hilltop towns.

### A few suggestions on how to spend a day in Paris:

- One of the most famous attractions in the city, **Promenade des Anglais** is a lovely 4.5 mile long promenade which runs from the airport to Castle Hill. Go for a stroll along "the Prom" and enjoy spectacular views of the azure Mediterranean Sea.
- With its narrow cobblestone streets, colourful facades, art galleries, and cute cafes, **Nice Old Town (le Vieux Nice)** can be easily explored on foot. Discover picturesque city squares such as Place du Palais de Justice, Place Rossetti and Place Saint François. Travellers can also stop by the famous **Cours Saleya (flower market)** and visit **Musée du Palais Lascaris** to see more than 500 musical instruments.
- Standing at 93 metres above sea level, **Parc de la Colline du Château** is a beautiful medieval castle in the centre of Nice. Climb to the summit to enjoy some seriously awesome views of the city and the Mediterranean Sea.

- Indulge in some retail therapy at **Avenue Jean Médecin**, the main shopping street in the city.
- Museum lovers can spend a few hours at the **Modern and Contemporary Art Museum (MAMAC)**. Expect to find more than 1,300 works including paintings by artists such as Andy Warhol, Martial Raysse and Jacques Villeglé.

**A couple of suggestions for day trips from Nice:**

Popular tourist destinations such as **Monaco** and **Cannes** are just a short drive away from Nice. Hop on a train to the pretty coastal towns of **Villefranche-sur-Mer** and **Menton**.

**Traditional foods to try:**

**Pissaladière** is a tasty pie with onions and anchovies.
**Salade niçoise** is made with tomatoes, lettuce, fresh green beans, hard-boiled eggs, tuna and olive oil.

**How to get to the city from the airport:**

You will land at Nice Côte d'Azur Airport. With a fast direct tramway line, getting to the city centre from the airport in Nice is easy. Find the Tram 2 line right in front of the terminal. The tramway runs approximately every 10 minutes and journey time is

30 minutes. Get your tickets from the machine right on the tram platform. You can pay by cash and with credit card.

## Lille

Nestled in northern France, Lille is celebrated for its well-preserved architecture, thriving food scene and charming squares dotted with baroque buildings. Whether you wish to get lost in the cobblestone streets of Vieux Lille, see esteemed works by Monet and Raphael or haggle with vendors at a lively open-air food market, there is much to look forward to when visiting Lille.

**A few suggestions on how to spend a day in Lille:**

- Commence with a visit to the old town **(Vieux Lille)**. With its cobblestone streets lined with colourful buildings, walk down the beautiful Rue de la Monnaie and discover colourful squares like **Place Louise de Bettignies**.
- Art lovers visiting Lille can spend a few hours at **Palais des Beaux-Arts**. One of the largest museums in the region, Palais des Beaux-Arts is home to works by artists such as Van Gogh, Rubens, Donatello, Monet and Picasso. The museum is situated inside a charming palace from the 19th century.

- How about a visit to a museum that is set in a former indoor swimming pool? Welcome to **La Piscine Museum,** a wonderful museum that houses a large archive of textile samples from the 19th and 20th century. It is a great place to learn more about Lille's industrial past.
- Situated within Citadelle Park, **Parc Zoologique** de Lille is home to a diverse range of animals from across the globe. Visitors will have a chance to spot lions, pandas and giraffes.
- Sports fans visiting Lille for a day or two should check out **Stade Pierre-Mauroy**. This swish new stadium is home to the local Lille OSC football team. In the summer season, the stadium doubles as a concert arena.
- Wish to enjoy panoramic views of the city? Listed as a UNESCO World Heritage site, the **Belfry** is an iconic tower in Lille. Climb the spiral staircase to enjoy spectacular vistas of the city. You will also a find a small museum which showcases the tower's rich heritage.

**How to reach Lille by Eurostar train:**
The Eurostar train runs directly from London to Lille in just under 1 hour and 30 minutes.

**Getting to the city from the airport:**

Lille Airport is located just 3 miles from the city in the small town of Lesquin.

The airport has its own direct bus route which connects the airport with Lille-Flandres railway station. Find the bus stop by entrance door 1. Shuttle buses leave once an hour in both directions and the journey lasts 20 minutes. Bus tickets can only be bought directly from the bus driver with cash/card.

## Bordeaux

The world's red wine capital, Bordeaux is a charming UNESCO-listed port city also known for its chic art galleries, exquisite architecture and cool museums.

**A few suggestions on how to spend a day in Bordeux:**

- Discover the **Old Town** of Bordeaux and its 18th and 19th-century classical and neoclassical buildings, avenues and picturesque squares. Don't miss **Place de la Comédie**, an elegant square that is home to the iconic **Grand Théâtre de Bordeaux**.
- Oenophiles will want to visit **La Cité du Vin**, an ultra-modern wine museum located on the banks of the Garonne River. Learn about the history of wine and how it is made through interactive screens and games. La Cité du Vin also has a nice restaurant, brasserie, and a wine shop. End your visit on the eighth floor with a glass of local wine and panoramic views of the city.
- Art lovers will not be bored in Bordeaux. Designed by Danish architect Bjarke Ingels, **Frac Nouvelle-**

**Aquitaine MÉCA** is a contemporary art museum that houses cutting-edge exhibitions. This extraordinary museum by the river also has a lovely terrace with splendid views across the city.

- A modern food hall on Quai de Bacalan, **Les Halles de Bacalan** is a mecca for foodies. Expect to find more than 20 merchants selling everything from local wines to fresh seafood and cured meats.
- Satisfy your shopping cravings on the longest pedestrian shopping street in all of Europe, the famous **Rue Sainte-Catherine**. From high-end international chain stores to French boutiques and small bargain shops, there is something for everyone.
- The harbour of Bordeaux, **Port de la Lune** and its surrounding area is a UNESCO World Heritage Site. It is a great spot for a walk or to sit and people watch. Travellers can also hire a bicycle and cycle along the river.

**Traditional foods to try in Bordeaux:**

**Arcachon Bay Oysters** are fresh local oysters that are delivered swiftly from Arcachon Bay.
**Canelé** is the beloved Bordeaux pastry.

**How to get from the airport to the city centre:**

Bordeaux–Mérignac Airport is the international airport of Bordeaux. The best way to reach the city centre is by tram. Take tram A to Bordeaux city centre (Place Pey Berland). The airport tram stop is located in front of the arrivals terminal between Hall A and Hall B. The tram leaves the airport every 10 minutes and takes approximately 40 minutes to reach the city centre. Purchase your tickets from the ticket machine right in front of the tram stop.

## Marseille

A melting pot of African and French culture, Marseille is a pleasant Mediterranean port city in the south of France. With an historic old town, vibrant culture and art galleries, this seaside city has plenty to offer.

**A few suggestions on how to spend a day in Marseille:**

- The **Vieux Port** (Old Harbour) is the place to start. Visit the **Sainte Marie Lighthouse**, explore the **Museum of Old Marseille** (home to marine artefacts) and unwind with a refreshing drink outside to soak up the views.
- You will find **Fort Saint-Jean** on the edge of the old harbour. Snap a photo in front of this 16th-century fortification which is one of the most iconic monuments of the city.
- Don't miss **Le Panier**, the old town. With its buildings adorned with shuttered windows and tempting artisanal shops, this is one of the

most picturesque neighbourhoods in southern France.
- For a better understanding of Mediterranean civilisations and history, visit the **Museum of Civilizations of Europe and the Mediterranean (MuCEM)**. Spread across three buildings, this eclectic museum houses everything from exhibitions to mini films.
- Art lovers should check out **Musée des Beaux-Arts**. Situated inside a beautiful palace, the gallery is home to paintings and sculptures created by Provencal and Italian artists.
- Located just off the coast, **Château d'If** is an iconic fort that can be visited by boat from the Vieux Port. Visitors will discover the history of this 16th century castle which was also used as a prison for political enemies of the state.
- Sports fans visiting Marseille can visit the largest club football stadium in France, the legendary **Stade Vélodrome**. **Olympique de Marseille's** home stadium offers an hour-long guided tour. Expect to see everything from the dressing rooms to the peaks of the terraces.

**Traditional foods to try in Marseille:**

**Bouillabaiss**e is a fish and seafood stew with wine, olive oil and saffron.
**Madeleines** are shell-shaped sweet pastries.

**Getting to the city centre from the airport:**

Marseille Provence Airport is the main international airport. The easiest way to reach the city centre is with a direct shuttle bus.

The bus leaves every 15 minutes and the journey time from the airport to the Marseille main train station is 25 minutes. This direct shuttle bus departs from platform 3 in front of the airport. Purchase your tickets from the ticket machine.

## Toulouse

With its trademark pink terracotta buildings, Toulouse is also known as 'La Ville Rose' (The Pink City). Whether you wish to walk down the enchanting Vieux Quartier (Old Quarter), snap a photo in front of picturesque Pont Neuf (New Bridge) or try delicious local foods at Marché Victor Hugo, Toulouse has a lot to offer.

**A few suggestions on how to spend a day in Toulouse:**

- Widely considered one of the most beautiful squares in France, **Le Place du Capitole** is the main square in Toulouse. Lined with outdoor terraces and restaurants, it is home to the **Town Hall** of Toulouse and the Capitole Theatre. This charming square frequently hosts events such as wine tastings, gardening fairs and Christmas markets.
- **Rue d'Alsace Lorraine** is the main shopping street in Toulouse. It is also a great place to

admire the beauty of Haussmann architecture and buildings like the Grand Hôtel Tivollier and Musée des Augustins.
- The city of Toulouse lies on the **Garonne River**. Go for a walk on the promenade along the river's banks and enjoy magnificent sunset views, picturesque bridges and public parks. Travellers can also hop on a river cruise to observe attractions such as the dome of **La Grave** and **Pont Neuf** from a different angle.
- Dating back to the 16th century, **Pont Neuf** is the oldest bridge in the city. It is also one of the most photographed places in Toulouse. Head to the left bank of the River Garonne for the best pics of this magical bridge.
- If you are into art, visit the amazing contemporary art museum in Toulouse called **Les Abattoirs**. Once a slaughterhouse, the museum houses awesome exhibitions of both international and French artists. Visiting with the little ones? Les Abattoirs has a cool corner for kids, as well as a carousel that you will find just outside the main entrance.
- The city's main market, **Marché Victor Hugo** is a good place to discover the local food specialties. From seafood and pastries to poultry and charcuterie, this market has it all. The ground floor is where you will find local vendors selling veggies, fruits, fish, meats and cheeses. On the second floor, visitors will find

many restaurants that serve local delicacies from the region.
- A very hip, young neighbourhood featuring narrow streets lined with bars, coffee shops and boutiques, **Carmes** is a great place to spend the afternoon and soak up the cosmopolitan vibe.
- Nature lovers staying for a day or two should not leave the city before experiencing **Jardin des Plantes.** The most popular park in the city is traversed by a stream that is frequented by swans, geese and ducks and features a pleasing selection of statues and water features dotted around.
- One of the oldest functioning canals in Europe, **Canal de Midi** is an enchanting place with centuries-old trees and rustic bridges. Cycling around this UNESCO World Heritage site in the morning or just before sunset is one of the most romantic things to do in Toulouse.

**Getting to the city from the airport:**

The city is served by Toulouse Blagnac Airport. The easiest way to get to the city centre is on a shuttle bus which runs every 20 minutes and takes approximately 25 minutes to reach Toulouse Matabiau station.

The shuttle bus station is located on the airport's ground floor close to gate C. Obtain tickets from the ticket machines located next to the Bus Station, buy them online or as you enter the shuttle bus.

## Belgium

### Brussels

Brussels is a city of great architecture, fascinating history and delicious moules marinières (mussels). With the benefit of a direct and fast Eurostar train from London, Brussels is a good option for a short stay.

**A few recommendations on how to spend a day in Brussels:**

- Start your visit at the **Grand Palace**. Surrounded by the 15th-century City Hall and other Gothic and Baroque-style buildings, the Grand Place is a UNESCO-listed cobblestone square known for its stunning architecture.
- Brussels is home to one of the most bizarre statues in Belgium, the statue of **Manneken Pis**. Dating back to the 17th century, the 'Little Man Pee' is popular with photographers.

- Another quirky attraction in Brussels is the famous **Atomium**. Over 100 metres tall, this weird silver structure is home to nine spherical rooms where you can see history and air travel exhibitions. The surrounding parkland is pretty.
- At the foot of the Atomium find '**Mini Europe**', a miniature park featuring reproductions of monuments located throughout Europe at a scale of 1:25. Approximately 80 cities and 350 buildings are displayed and are accompanied by live action models such as trains, cable cars and an erupting volcano. Charges apply.
- Situated inside a beautiful Renaissance-style arcade from the mid-1800s, **Les Galeries Royales Saint-Hubert** is a mecca for shoppers but is equally pleasant to just admire the architecture. This glass-roof arcade also has theatres, art galleries, and a few restaurants.
- **Musee Royaux Des Beaux Arts** is an ideal destination for all art lovers visiting Brussels. This fabulous museum is home to a vast collection of modern and ancient art. Expect to see works by artists like Rubens, Van Dyke and Memling.

**Getting to the city centre from the airport:**

Brussels-Zaventem Airport serves the city of Brussels. The easiest way to get to the city centre is by train. The railway station is located directly under the airport building. Just take the lift from the arrivals hall down to the platform. Train tickets can be bought from the ticket machines or via the Belgium Rail website. Trains run every 10 minutes to the journey to the city centre from the airport is approximately 20 minutes.

## How to reach Brussels by Eurostar train:

Travel time from London to Brussels by Eurostar train is only 2 hours. Depart from London St Pancras to Brussels Midi through the Channel Tunnel.

## Antwerp

Antwerp, a vibrant port city associated with international diamond trading, boasts gourmet delights of both superior chocolatiers and Michelin star restaurants. Belgium's second-largest city also has a picturesque and historic centre.

## A few recommendations on how to spend a day in Brussels:

- Antwerp has one of the most exquisite railway stations in Europe. **Antwerp Central Station** is a grand train station known for its Neo-Renaissance and Art Nouveau architecture. Pop inside to admire the beauty of this giant structure of marble, steel and glass.
- You will find the world's largest Belgian chocolate museum just across the street from

the railway station. **Chocolate Nation** is a place where you can learn about the history of chocolate, see how it is made and sample some.

- Your next stop is the famous **Meir Shopping Street**. Stretching from the central train station to the **Cathedral of Our Lady**, this shopping street is lined with luxury boutiques and world-famous European brands. **Stadsfeestzaal** is the most famous shopping mall on this street.
- Antwerp's **Ferris wheel**, called 'The View', offers a fun way to survey the city's landmark buildings and river mouth from semi-enclosed gondolas. With a bird's eye view, you will be poised to take perfect photos.
- Spread across 10 hectares, **Antwerp Botanical Garden** is home to nearly 7,000 plant species. Visitors will find exotic plants and trees as well as shrubs and herbs at this world-class botanical garden.
- Visit **the Royal Museum of Fine Arts** to admire a large collection of tapestries, paintings and sculptures dating back hundreds of years.
- Beer lovers must experience Antwerp's famous **De Koninck Antwerp City Brewery** complete with interactive exhibitions, audio-visual displays and themed rooms.
- The home of Peter Paul Rubens, the **Ruben House Museum (Rubenshuis)** is packed

with a bunch of works created by the famous Flemish painter.

## How to get from the airport to the city centre:

Antwerp Airport is 4 miles from the city centre. The easiest way to travel between the airport and 'Antwerpen Berchem' railway station is via bus routes 51, 52 or 53 from Antwerp Airport. Tickets can be bought from the ticket machines or via SMS. These buses run every 15 minutes.

Visitors will find the bus stop (Deurne Luchthaven) in front of the airport building. When you reach 'Antwerpen Berchem' railway station, change to tram number 9 to 'Groenplaats' Metro to reach the city centre in 6 minutes. This tram departs every 8 minutes.

### Bruges

A real feast for the eyes, Bruges resembles a medieval fairytale town. From pretty squares and beautifully paved streets to museums and canal boats, this small city is brimming with charm.

**A few recommendations on how to spend a day in Bruges:**

- A sweeping piazza surrounded by intricate architecture, start your day at the **Market Square**. Some of the most notable attractions include the historic **Craenenberg Café** and the **Hof building**.

- Often referred to as the 'Venice of the North', Bruges is famous for its beautiful canals. There are many waterways that cut through the city and one of the best things to do is to hop on one of the **canal boat tours**. These boat tours last for about 30 minutes and allow you to admire the abundant statues, Renaissance buildings, and picturesque bridges from a low vantage point. It is a great way to see the city if you are short on time.
- The **Tolkeinesque Belfort** building is one of the most famous attractions in the city. Those who climb the (slightly claustrophobic) stairway to the top of the tower will be rewarded with panoramic views of the city.
- To learn more about the art history of Flemish and Belgian paintings, pay a visit to the **Groeninge Museum**. It houses an impressive collection of 18th and 19th-century neoclassical pieces, as well as Flemish and Belgian paintings.
- How about a visit to a museum dedicated to fries? Bruges is home to the eccentric **Frietmuseum**. Situated inside a beautiful 14th century building, the museum explores the history, cultural significance and production of Belgian fries. Visitors will have the opportunity to taste authentic Belgian fries in the museum's cellar during the guided tour.
- If you like beer, a visit to the **De Halve Maan** brewery in Bruges is a must. It is best to book

the guided 45-minute tour a few days before your trip. Those who are short on time can visit the outdoor beer garden at the brewery.
- The **Lovers' Bridge** and **Lake of Love** is for all your romantics visiting Bruges. A haven of peace and tranquillity, this public green space is home to a lovely castle and a magnificent bridge. The locals say that if you kiss your partner on this bridge, your love will last forever.

**How to get from the airport to the city centre:**

Travellers arriving at Brussels-Zaventem Airport can take a direct train to Bruges. The journey takes about an hour.

**How to reach Bruges by Flight/Eurostar train:**

The fast Eurostar train from London to Brussels is a great means of reaching Bruges. From Brussels, change to a local Belgian SNCB train to reach Bruges.

## The Netherlands

### Amsterdam

Amsterdam, as the capital of the Netherlands, is packed with tons to see and do. Thanks to her compact size, 90% of the city's highlights are within a 30-minute walk. The extensive network of canals is frequently crisscrossed by flower-covered bridges and lined with elegant canal houses which makes for scenic strolls.

**A few suggestions on how to spend a day:**

- Art enthusiasts can marvel at varied works in the **Rijksmuseum** and **Van Gogh Museum**.
- **Anne Frank's house** is a must-see for many visitors, but advance booking is essential.
- Football fans would love to take a behind-the-scenes tour of AFC Ajax's legendary home (the Netherlands's largest stadium): The **Johan Cruijff ArenA Stadium**. It is best reached by metro 50 and 54 from Central Station, 18 mins.
- A new **5D flight experience** called **"This is Holland"** in the north of the city takes visitors on a 90-minute ride to experience highlights of other locations in the Netherlands. While seated in a flight-simulator type chair, multi-sensory effects such as smells, movement and sound are used. Take the free ferry with destination "Buiksloterweg" from the rear of Central Station, across the street from the taxi rank. By walking towards the Amsterdam Tower (the tallest building on that side of the city) the attraction can be reached in 8 minutes.
- Beer drinkers could be tempted by the **Heineken Experience:** set inside the former Heineken brewery visitors can learn about the brewing process, the brand's heritage and round off with two chilled beers.

- **Canal boat sightseeing tours** offer an alternative angle to view the city from and audio guides narrate a range of interesting historical nuggets as the boats traverse the vast network of canals.
- The infamous red-light district makes for an eye-opening walk at any time of day or night. **Red Light Secrets -Museum of Prostitution** offers a short but thorough insight into the district for anyone curious about the area and how the long -regulated trade operates as an integral part of Amsterdam.

**Traditional foods to try:**

**Stroopwafel** is deliciously sweet comprising a thin waffle with inner syrup layer.
**Herring** is a popular street food- served simply with pickles and onions or as part of a sandwich.

**How to get from the airport to the city centre:**

Amsterdam's huge airport is Schipol, served by a range of budget airlines.

The train is the easiest way to reach Amsterdam's Central Station, taking approximately 15 minutes.

Find the NS railway station directly below the terminal building via the escalator or lift. Tickets must be purchased before boarding from the ticket machines and validated by holding the ticket against one of the validation poles that display the blue NS arrow logo on a yellow background.

### How to reach Amsterdam by Eurostar train:

The Eurostar travels direct from London to Amsterdam Central Station in just under four hours.

### Rotterdam

The second-largest city in the Netherlands, Rotterdam is not your typical Dutch city. Rotterdam features ultra-modern skyscrapers, food markets, museums and quirky architecture.

### A few suggestions on how to spend a day:

- The best views of Rotterdam can be enjoyed from the top of the **Euromast Tower**. Standing 185 metres above ground, it is the tallest building in the city. Climb to the top for some seriously awesome views.
- Rotterdam's unique **Cube Houses** are known for their quirky cube-shaped upper storeys. Each cube designed by the famous Dutch architect Piet Blom is nestled atop a hexagonally shaped base. Travellers can visit the **Show Cube**, a fully furnished cube house that serves as a museum. It also contains information about the history of the buildings.
- Right opposite the Cube Houses is the legendary **Market Hall** with its distinctive arch shape encrusted with a large grey glass exterior. It is the best culinary destination in the city with more than 100 food stalls, restaurants and bars offering both Dutch and international foods.
- If you are looking for a family-friendly tourist attraction in Rotterdam, spend a few hours at the renowned **Rotterdam Zoo** (or **Diergaarde Blijdorp**). You will have a chance to see animals such as giraffes, polar bears, penguins, rhinos, gorillas and tigers.
- Museum lovers can stop by **Kunsthal Rotterdam** which houses rotating exhibits of all types of art and photography. To see a museum dedicated to fashion and design, check out **Het Nieuwe Instituut**. There is

also the **Natural History Museum** where you will find fossils and skeletons.

- The city is strung around the Nieuwe Maas river, making it an ideal destination for boat tours.
- Spend a few hours walking through charming **Delfshaven** which is known for its traditional Dutch pubs, mills, and flower-lined canals.

**How to get from the airport to the city centre:**

Rotterdam's closest airport is The Hague Airport. The local transport company RET provides public transportation between The Hague Airport and Rotterdam Centraal railway station.

Take bus route 33 which runs every 10 minutes from the airport. The bus stops right outside the airport terminal. Travel time between the airport and the city centre is 20 minutes. Buy your tickets from the ticket machines at the airport bus station.

**How to reach Rotterdam by Eurostar train:**

Eurostar train runs directly from London to Amsterdam via Rotterdam. It takes just 3 hours and 29 minutes to get from London St Pancras to Rotterdam Central Station via Eurostar train.

### Eindhoven

Eindhoven is a city of technology, innovation and design. Nicknamed 'Lichtstad' (City of Light), it is associated with its vibrant arts and culture scene, hip cafes, an awesome football stadium and world-class museums.

**A few suggestions on how to spend a day in Eindhoven:**

- The history of the city is linked with the Phillips Company and **Philipsmuseum** is a good place to start your Eindhoven travel itinerary. See inventions and products of Philips with interactive exhibits and kids' workshops.
- Welcome to the **Van Abbemuseum**, one of the most important galleries of modern and contemporary art in the country. Visitors can look forward to seeing nearly 2,800 artworks ranging from paintings by Pablo Picasso to numerous sculptures and art installations.
- Shaped like a UFO, **Evoluon** is definitely the strangest building in the city. Once an interactive science museum, Evoluon nowadays operates as a conference venue. Admire the beauty of this absurd building from the outside or check out the RetroFuture exhibition that shows how folk from the past anticipated the future to look like.
- Sports fans visiting Eindhoven should not miss the home of PSV Eindhoven, the **Phillips Football Stadium**. Tours of the stadium are available and include photos and film footage of career highlights, team practices, historic outfits, artefacts and much more.

- Your last stop for the day is the **Het Veem Food Market**. Located in the the **Strijp-S**, this food market is a great spot to sample local cuisine.
- Along the road from the bus station is the **Silly Walk Tunnel** - a must for Monty Python fans as you get to 'walk' the length of the free tunnel with John Clees. It is difficult to resist copying his comical stances as they change constantly along the wall.

**How to get from the airport to the city centre:**

Eindhoven Airport is small, meaning that minimal time is wasted getting from the plane itself to clearing the airport. The easiest way to get from Eindhoven Airport to the city centre is via the number 400 or 401 bus. The journey time is 25 minutes and the buses depart just outside of the arrivals hall.

Both buses have Airport Shuttle printed on them, so spotting them is easy. These buses run every 15 minutes and tickets can be purchased from the bus driver or via ticket machines that are located at the bus station and at the baggage reclaim area.

**<u>Eastern Europe</u>**

# Hungary

## Budapest

Hungary's capital, Budapest, is a city of brilliant architecture, fabulous thermal baths and island parks. Whatever your interests, this city on the banks of the Danube River offers stacks of exciting things to do and see.

**A few suggestions on how to spend a day in Budapest:**

- Take the **funicular** from Clark Ádám tér to reach the picturesque **Buda Castle** in Budim.
- Explore the **Jewish Quarter** and its popular ruined bars inside abandoned buildings.
- **Gellert Bat and Spa Centre** is one of the best places to unwind and enjoy swimming pools, saunas, plunge pools and massage treatments. This popular thermal bath is situated inside a beautiful Art Nouveau-style building.
- With its steam and dry saunas, whirlpool, relaxation areas, and massage centres, **Széchenyi Baths** is the most popular thermal bath in the city. On the weekend, this place transforms into an outdoor swimming pool party venue with light shows and DJs.
- **Fisherman's Bastion** is in the historic district of Castle Hill and is known for its neo-Gothic terrace that offers panoramic views of the city.

- In the middle of the Danube, **Margaret Island** has stacks of green spaces, recreational facilities, bike paths, cafes and restaurants. This 1.5 mile long island also features an unmissable musical fountain attraction.
- Shopaholics visiting Budapest can spend a few hours on **Andrássy Avenue**. From major brands situated inside neo-Renaissance townhouses to small local boutiques selling handmade souvenirs, this famous street offers something for everyone.
- To see medieval Hungarian art, artefacts from ancient Egypt and a raft of famous European paintings, visit the **Museum of Fine Art.**
- A **night cruise on the Danube River** allows you to admire the beauty of lit-up tourist attractions from a unique perspective. From a classic boat tour to an all-inclusive five-star dining experience cruise or a booze river tour, there are many Danube River cruises to choose from in Budapest.

**How to get from the airport to the city centre:**

Budapest Airport is the main international airport in Budapest. Take bus number 100E to reach the city centre. This bus runs every 30 minutes and the journey time from the airport to the city centre is approximately 40 minutes. The bus stop is between the terminal buildings on the arrivals level.

Purchase tickets from the airport kiosk, ticket machines, the bus driver or via the BKK mobile app.

# Slovakia

## Bratislava

With a picturesque medieval old town and a blend of Baroque, Gothic, and Soviet architecture, Bratislava will enchant travellers with its cultural attractions and historic landmarks.

**A few suggestions on how to spend a day in Bratislava:**
- A good place to start is the Old Town. As you amble through charming streets lined with medieval buildings, you will find the picturesque **Hlavne Namestie (Main Square)**. Do also check out the nearby **Stara Radnica (courtyard of the old town hall)**. Some of the best-preserved streets to roam around include Panska and Mickalska.
- Towering above the Old Town, **Bratislava Castle** now acts as the **Museum of History**. To enjoy incredible views of the city and the Danube River, climb the 47-metre-high **Crown Tower**.
- The **Blue Church** (Church of St. Elizabeth of Hungary) is one of the most unique churches in Eastern Europe. Known for its blue-coloured exterior and art-nouveau architectural style, the Blue Church is sure to impress.
- Officially called the **Bridge of the Slovak National Uprising, UFO** is one of the most recognisable symbols of the city. As the name

suggests, it is shaped like a UFO. You can take the lift to the **Observation Deck** from which you can enjoy sweeping views over Bratislava. Travellers can also have a memorable dining experience at the onsite restaurant.

- With 4,000 different species of plants, the **Botanical Gardens of Comenius University** is a great place to spend an hour or two. It is open from April and October and houses attractions such as the Palm House, the Japanese Gardens and the Cactus Greenhouse. Don't miss the Rosarium with 120 rose species.

**Traditional foods to try:**

**Bryndzové Halušky** is dumplings with sheep's cheese.
**Zemiakové placky** is a potato pancake with flour and garlic.
**Šišky** are fried dumplings with marmalade and sugar.

**How to get from the airport to the city centre:**

Bratislava M. R. Štefánik Airport is located 10 miles from the centre of Bratislava. The best way to reach the city centre is via bus number 61. You will find the bus station right outside the main terminal building.

Bus 61 departs every 10 minutes from the airport and takes about 30 to 45 minutes to reach the city centre. Tickets are available at the terminal and the bus stop. After buying your ticket, you need to validate it on board the bus.

# Czechia (Czech Republic)

## Prague

The capital of the Czechia (formerly known as the Czech Republic), Prague is known for its stunning historical architecture, statue-lined bridges, world-class museums and great beer.

**A few suggestions on how to spend a day in Prague:**

- Prague possesses many historical sites such as the **Old Town Square, the Astronomical Clock,** and **Prague Castle**. In fact, the historical centre of the city is one giant UNESCO World Heritage List. Stroll through the historical streets of the Old Town and pause at the square to watch various street performers, musicians and merchants.
- Nestled on the Vltava River, **Charles Bridge** is one of the city's iconic attractions. Amble across this 14th-century bridge clad with striking statues and enjoy magnificent city views.
- Culture vultures will want to spend a few hours in the **Jewish District**, also known as **Josefov**. Located between the river and the Old Town, this district boasts significant historical buildings including six beautiful synagogues.

- Your next stop should be the **Castle District** where you will find the breathtaking **Prague Castle**. Some of the main attractions at the castle include the St Vitus Cathedral, the Basilica of St George and Golden Lane. Purchase the 'skip the line' tickets and enjoy an informative 2.5-hour guided tour.
- There is no shortage of fabulous museums in Prague. **The National Museum** on Wenceslas Square is worth visiting, as is the **Dox Gallery** in the Holešovice district.
- Nature lovers will enjoy the wonderful parks such as **Letna Park, Riegrovy Sady**, and **Havlíčkovy Sady**.
- If you are visiting for just a day and want to see all the major tourist attractions, hop on **Tram number 42**. This hop-on-hop-off service features characterful vintage trams.
- Prague is known for its amazing puppet shows. Catch puppet performances at the **National Marionette Theatre** and **Theatre Spejbla & Hurvinek**.
- Join a **cruise on the River Vltava** to experience many historical buildings and monuments from a unique perspective.

**How to get from the airport to the city centre:**

Prague Airport's AE Express bus service is the most convenient way to reach the city centre. Find the AE Express bus stops just outside terminals 1 and 2.

Purchase bus tickets online, directly from the driver or at the Prague Airport Info Centre. Buses depart every 30-60 minutes depending on the time of day. It takes around 25 to 40 minutes to reach the city centre.

## Romania

### Bucharest

Bucharest is a vibrant city where high-rise towers, Byzantine architecture and brutalist Communist-era apartment blocks form an intriguing blend. From a replica of the Arc de Triomphe to one of the most beautiful bookstores in the world, Bucharest promises plenty to interest visitors.

**A few suggestions on how to spend a day in Burcharest:**

- **Centrul Vechi (the Old Town)** is small but unmissable. This stylish pedestrian zone features small, cobbled alleys lined with hipster coffee shops, historic sites, restaurants and boutiques.
- If you are short on time, ride **the hop-on-hop-off bus** which stops at 13 of the most popular and significant landmarks in the city. These buses depart every 15 minutes and a free guided tour of the Old Town is included in the ticket.
- With a mix of Modernist, Art Nouveau and Soviet architecture, the capital of Romania has

astonishing architectural diversity. Architecture lovers should not miss sites such as the **Cantacuzino Palace**, the **Central Library**, and the **Coltea Hospital**.

- Located in the Old Town, Cărture☐ti **Carousel Bookstore** is one of the world's most beautiful and beloved bookstores. Situated inside a charming 19th-century building, the bookstore occupies 6 floors and over 1,000 square metres of space. Find nearly 10,000 books, as well as a decent collection of CDs and DVDs.
- Nature lovers should stop at **Herăstrău Park**. Built around a lake, it boasts a range of sculptures. Enjoy a boat ride on the lake.
- Snap a photo in front of the **Pasajul Victoria passage**, also known as the colourful **Umbrella Street**.
- Art lovers should not miss **the National Museum of Art**. The **Museum of Natural History** with its definitive dinosaur skeletons is also worth checking out.

**Traditional foods to try:**

**Sarmale cu Mamaliguta** is stuffed cabbage rolls with polenta.
**Papanasi cu Smîntînă** are cheese doughnuts with sweet cream.

**Getting from the airport to the city centre:**

The best way to reach the city centre from Bucharest Henri Coanda airport is on the 100 Express Bus route. The bus stop is in front of the terminal building and the buses run every 15 minutes, taking between 24-40 minutes depending on traffic. Purchase tickets at the ticket machines and make a contactless card payment.

## Southern Europe

### Spain

### Madrid

The capital of Spain, Madrid is a city renowned for impressive palaces and an abundance of art museums. Constantly buzzing with activity, this vibrant city is packed with an array of cultural attractions.

**A few suggestions on how to spend a day in Madrid:**

- Inside the **Prado Museum** of Spanish art, you will find a fabulous collection of masterpieces from artists such as Rubens and El Greco.
- Located next to the Prado Museum, the **Real Jardín Botánico (Royal Botanical Garden)** offers features such as splendid sculptures, and impressive greenhouses. The oldest botanical garden in Europe is also home to the **Museum of Natural History.**
- Art lovers should explore **Reina Sofia**, a contemporary, modern art museum. Don't

miss Picasso's iconic anti-war painting "Guernica".

- Culture vultures should not miss the **Royal Palace** in Madrid. With attractions such as the Royal Chapel, the Throne Room and the Royal Apothecary, it is one of the most majestic palaces of Europe. The sumptuous décor inside the palace is spectacular.
- **Plaza Mayor** is a beautiful square known for its grand **statue of King Philip III** which was designed by Giambologna. Take your pick of bars, restaurants and shops here. You can also stop by **Puerta del Sol**, a lively square located in the heart of Madrid. Spot the legendary **Bear and the Strawberry Tree statue.**
- Foodies visiting Madrid for a day or two will want to check out the lively **San Miguel Market**. Situated inside a historic building just west of Plaza Mayor are dozens of vendors offering local specialities such as goat's cheese, seafood tapas and Iberian ham.
- Football fans can join a tour of the iconic **Estadio Santiago Bernabéu**, home of Real Madrid. The stadium also has a well-designed museum featuring permanent and temporary exhibitions, team artefacts and trophies.

**Getting from the airport to the city centre:**

The best way to reach the city centre from Adolfo Suárez Madrid-Barajas Airport is via the EMT Airport

Express bus service. The bus, number 203, is yellow and runs 24 hours a day from the airport to the city centre. Find bus stops at terminals T1, T2, and T4. If you arrive at terminal T3, a free airport shuttle connects it to the other terminals. These buses leave every 15 to 20 minutes and travel time to the city centre is approximately 40 minutes. Tickets can be purchased on the bus (cash only).

## Barcelona

Barcelona is a city of elaborate architectural marvels, lush green spaces and exquisite food and wine. Whether you wish to explore the picturesque series of narrow streets and alleys of the Gothic Quarter, take a stroll along the busy Las Ramblas Boulevard or spend a day on the beach, the capital of Catalonia offers something for everyone.

**A few suggestions on how to spend a day in Barcelona:**

- Explore the Gothic Quarter with its medieval alleyways lined with looming churches, cute cafes and varied restaurants.
- Admire the beauty of Antoni Gaudí's masterpieces such as **Casa Milà**, **Casa Batlló**, **Casa Vicens**, and **La Sagrada Família**.
- Sample a variety of tapas and other local delicacies at the giant outdoor **Boqueria market**.

- Nature lovers can meander through the colourful **Park Güell** and see masterpieces such as the Dragon Fountain, Column Room, Gaudi House Museum and the Elephant Cave.
- Discover **Las Ramblas**, the wide, tree-lined pedestrian street packed with artists, terraces, restaurants, and flower stalls. This is one of the most popular attractions in the city.
- Appreciate nearly 4,000 works by Pablo Picasso at the **Picasso Museum**. Discover historical Catalan art from the including sculptures, paintings, photography, posters, and video pieces at **Catalonia's National Art Museum** (MNAC).
- Take the **funicular to Montjuïc** for some seriously awesome views of the city and an old castle to explore in extensive parkland.
- If the weather is nice, spend a few hours on the beach in Barcelona. The most popular beach in the city is **Barceloneta Beach**.
- If you have an extra day or two, hop on a train to Monserrat where you will find a charming **Benedictine Monastery**. The picturesque coastal town of **Sitges** is also just a short drive away from the capital of Catalonia.

**How to get to the city centre from the airport:**

Located approximately 9 miles from the city centre, Barcelona El Prat International Airport (BCN) is the main airport in the capital of Catalonia.

The best way to reach the city centre is via metro. The L9 metro line goes directly from El Prat airport to the city centre. This metro line runs every 10 minutes and takes around 30 minutes to reach the city centre. There are metro stations located both in Terminal 1 and Terminal 2. Get your tickets from automatic machines or customer service counters.

## Malaga

Malaga is a beautiful coastal city nestled in the south of Spain. From spending a day on the beach to exploring the museums on offer, there is plenty to keep you entertained in this vibrant Mediterranean city.

**A few suggestions on how to spend a day in Malaga:**

- **The Alcazaba** is the most iconic visitor attraction in Malaga. Built in the 11th century, this impressive cluster of old buildings (including a former Moorish palace) is a must-visit spot for history buffs.
- You will find the ruins of the **Roman Theatre** just below the Alcazaba. One of the very few surviving Roman ruins in the country, the Roman Theatre ruins are well-preserved and worth checking out. In this very spot, the

bloodthirsty Romans would watch gladiator fights. An interesting fact is that actor Antonio Banderas performed at this theatre as a child.

- Climb to the top of the charming **Gibralfaro Castle** to enjoy spectacular views of the city and the Strait of Gibraltar. It will take you around 30 minutes to reach this 14th-century castle.
- **La Concepción Jardín Botánico** is a beautiful botanical garden and one of the largest tropical gardens in all of Europe. Take the opportunity to spot over 25,000 species of plants and trees. Located a bit outside the city centre, to reach the garden's gates take bus number 2 from the centre of Malaga.
- There is no shortage of fabulous museums in Malaga. Learn about the life of Pablo Picasso and see some of his personal belongings at the **Picasso Birthplace Museum**. To admire the beauty of Spanish and Andalusian paintings, stop by the **Carmen Thyssen Museum**. There is also the **Flamenco Art Museum** which is dedicated to the traditional Spanish dance.
- The **Soho neighbourhood** was formerly a decaying district. Nowadays, it is a salubrious neighbourhood also known as the 'art district'. You will notice that many buildings are covered with cool art and graffiti. Expect to see everything from handicraft shops and hipster bars to local art galleries here.

- No visit to Malaga is complete without spending a few hours on the beach. The closest beach to the city centre is **Malagueta**. To escape the crowds in the summer season, head a little further out to **El Palo Beach**.
- Foodies visiting Malaga for a day or two can stop by **Mercado Central de Atarazanas**. Housed inside a majestic historical building that was previously a military fort, the market offers a vast array of culinary treats: everything from pinchitos and tapas to international foods.

### How to get to the city centre from the airport:

Malaga-Costa del Sol Airport is located 5 miles from the centre of Malaga. The best way to reach the city centre from the airport is with the "A" Express Bus service. The bus stop is located on the ground floor of Terminal 1 and you can obtain a ticket outside the terminal or from the bus driver (who will only accept cash). The bus will take between 15-25 minutes to reach the centre.

There is also the option of taking a new train line at the airport. The underground train station is located opposite the exit of the arrivals area at Terminal 3 and Line C1 departs every 20 minutes. You can purchase tickets in the ticket hall at Terminal 3. It will take about 12 minutes to reach the centre of Malaga on the train.

## Seville

Positioned in the heart of Andalusia, Seville is a city that blends history, culture and traditions. With its rich Moorish heritage, lively festivals and passionate flamenco performances, Seville captures the essence of southern Spanish culture. A day or two in Seville promises to be an adventure to remember.

**A few suggestions on how to spend a day in Seville:**

- Begin your journey with a visit to the **Alcazar**, a UNESCO World Heritage site that transports you back in time to the era of Moorish rule. Marvel at the intricate Islamic architecture, lush gardens and ornate tilework.

- Adjacent to the Alcazar is the awe-inspiring **Seville Cathedral**, the largest Gothic cathedral in the world. The cathedral's interior, with its grandeur and religious artefacts, is truly impressive. Ascend the Giralda Tower for panoramic views of the city.
- Step into the charming lanes of **Barrio Santa Cruz**, the historic **Jewish quarter**. It is a place where narrow streets are dotted with beautiful whitewashed buildings. Quaint cafes and hidden squares add to the charm.
- No visit to Seville is complete without experiencing the passion of flamenco. Attend a **live flamenco show** at places such as **Tablao Flamenco El Palacio Andaluz, Tablao Flamenco Las Setas and Tablao Alvarez Quintero**.
- Escape the urban hustle at **Parque de Maria Luisa**, an expansive public park. Stroll through picturesque gardens, admire fountains and statues, or rent a rowboat on the Plaza de España's canal.
- For sports enthusiasts, catching a Real Betis football match at the **Benito Villamarin Stadium** is a thrilling experience.
- End your day with a visit to the **Metropol Parasol**, a modern architectural marvel in the heart of the city. The wooden structure provides panoramic views of Seville's skyline.

**A day out a little further afield:**

Have an extra day? Hop on a train to the city of **Cordoba**. The city is known for its splendid cathedral and manicured gardens.

**Getting to the City Centre from the Airport:**

Seville Airport is located 7 miles from the centre of the city. The easiest and most efficient way to reach the city centre is by taking the airport shuttle bus. The buses run every 30 minutes and the journey takes about 35 minutes. The bus stops outside the main arrivals door, on the left. Purchase your tickets on the bus when you board.

## Alicante

Positioned on the southeastern coast of Spain, Alicante is steeped in history yet also offers modern charms and sun-kissed beaches. Whether you wish to enjoy the crystal-clear waters of Postiguet Beach or attend a Flamenco performance, here are some options for travellers who wish to spend a day or two in this enchanting city.

**A few recommendations on how to spend a day in Alicante:**

- Perched high on **Mount Benacantil, Santa Bárbara Castle** offers panoramic views of Alicante and the Mediterranean Sea. History enthusiasts will revel in the castle's rich past, dating back to the 9th century.

- For a leisurely afternoon, wander along **Explanada de España**, a picturesque promenade fringed with palm trees and mosaics. This waterfront boulevard is frequented by local musicians, street artists and has plenty of appealing pavement cafes.
- Foodies visiting Alicante simply can't miss **Mercado Central**, the city's bustling central market. Here, you'll find a cornucopia of fresh produce, seafood, and local delicacies. Treat your taste buds to tapas, paella and turrón.
- Dive deeper into Alicante's history at the **Archaeological Museum.** The modern exhibits and interactive displays showcase the region's archaeological treasures, back from prehistoric times to the Islamic era.
- Beach enthusiasts will be keen to spend a few hours at **Postiguet Beach**. With its golden sands and crystal-clear waters, this urban beach offers a wide range of facilities.
- Immerse yourself in the passion of Spanish culture by attending a **Flamenco show**. Several venues in the city host these traditional performances.
- Sports fans should visit the football stadium **Estadio José Rico Pérez.**
- Discover the charming, narrow streets of **Barrio Santa Cruz**, the old quarter of Alicante. This historic neighbourhood, with its colourful houses and vibrant flowers, is a must-see district in the city.

**How to get to the city centre from the airport:**

Alicante-Elche Airport is where you will land when visiting Alicante. The most convenient way to reach the city centre is via the C-6 bus service. This bus service runs every 20 minutes and the journey time between the airport and the city centre is around 25 minutes.

You will find the C-6 bus stop located on the second floor, just outside the main building. Tickets can be purchased directly from the driver or at the automatic ticket machines at the airport.

## Italy

### Rome

Consistently ranked as one of the most visit-worthy destinations in Europe, Rome offers history, culture and romance in abundance. With its iconic landmarks, ancient ruins and delectable cuisine, the capital of Italy offers something for every type of traveller.

**A few suggestions on how to spend a day in Rome:**

- Begin your Roman adventure with a visit to the **Colosseum**, an architectural marvel that echoes the roars of gladiators and fierce beasts from days gone by. Explore the amphitheatre's underground tunnels and imagine the grandeur of ancient spectacles that once shaped one of the finest and oldest cities in the world.

- Step back in time as you wander through the **Roman Forum**, a vast archaeological site that served as the heart of ancient Rome. The Roman Forum is displays impressive ruins of temples and arches.
- No visit to Rome is complete without spending some time at **Vatican City** which is home to attractions such as **St. Peter's Basilica** and the **Sistine Chapel**. Marvel at Michelangelo's inspired frescoes beneath the basilica's dome.
- You haven't been to Rome unless you have made a wish at the **Trevi Fountain**. This Baroque masterpiece with its cascading waters and mythological sculptures is spectacular. Don't forget to throw a coin over your shoulder into the fountain, ensuring your return to Rome.
- **Trastevere** is a neighbourhood known for its Bohemian vibes and gastronomic delights. Cross the Tiber to this charming district. Explore artisan shops, sip espresso in a café and try authentic Roman cuisine at a local trattoria.
- Escape the urban hustle at the **Borghese Gallery**, a haven of art and greenery. Wander

through the landscaped gardens and admire the beauty of masterpieces by Caravaggio, Bernini and Raphael.
- Gaze at **Piazza Navona**, a grand square adorned with fountains and surrounded by elegant Baroque buildings. Street performers and outdoor cafes add to the atmosphere.

**How to get to the city centre from the airport:**

The main airport in Rome is Fiumicino Airport. If you land here, take the Leonardo Express to reach the city centre. The journey time is 32 minutes and trains run every 15 minutes. You can purchase bus tickets online or from ticket machines close to the platform.

However, Ciampino Airport is used by some budget airlines. The best option to reach the city centre from here is on a shuttle bus. Buses run 13 times a day and journey time is 40 minutes.

**Venice**

Venice is the ultimate romantic getaway: comprising meandering alleys, gondoliers, the majestic Grand Canal and beautifully preserved palaces and piazzas. Venice is a small city with most attractions located centrally, lending itself perfectly to a day trip.

**A few suggestions on how to spend a day in Venice:**

- **St. Mark's Basilica** is a marvel of Byzantine architecture. Admire the intricate mosaics that

adorn its interior. The panoramic views from the terrace are spectacular.
- Immerse yourself in the lively atmosphere of the **Rialto Bridge and Market**. The bridge, an iconic symbol of Venice, spans the Grand Canal and leads to a bustling market where you can sample fresh produce, local delicacies and handmade crafts.
- Delve into Venetian history at the **Doge's Palace**, a masterpiece of Gothic architecture. Explore the opulent rooms, the infamous **Bridge of Sighs** and the prison cells. This historical gem tells the story of the political and cultural heritage of Venice.
- No visit to Venice is complete without a romantic **gondola ride**. Drift along the serene canals, passing under charming bridges and past historic buildings. It's a quintessential Venetian experience that allows you to appreciate the city's unique beauty from a lower viewing point.
- For art enthusiasts, the **Peggy Guggenheim Collection** is a must-visit. Housed in the heiress's former residence, this museum showcases an impressive array of modern art, including works by Picasso and Dalí. The picturesque garden is also worth a look.
- Foodies will not want to miss the **Cicchetti Tasting Tour**. Indulge your taste buds in a tasting tour, exploring the local Venetian tradition of small, tapas-style dishes.

- Art lovers will want to spend an hour or two at **Gallerie dell'Accademia**. This world-famous museum hosts a magnificent collection of pre-19th-century art and shows works by world-renowned artists such as Canaletto and Bellini.

**A day out a little further afield:**

Visit **Murano and Burano Islands** on a boat trip. Murano is known for its exquisite glass craftsmanship, while Burano has vibrant, colourful houses.

**How to get from the airport to the city centre:**

Venice Marco Polo Airport is the main airport. Jump on bus number 5 which departs every 15 minutes. It takes approximately 20 minutes to reach the city centre. Bus 5 from the airport leaves from the bus terminal located just outside the arrivals hall, between Exits 1 and 2. Buy tickets online or from the machines.

### Florence

Deep in the heart of Tuscany, Florence's rich history and architectural wonders lie in wait behind every corner. Known as the 'Cradle of the Renaissance', this city is a mecca for art lovers. Whether you wish to admire Michelangelo's David at the Galleria dell'Accademia or sample local foods, there is much to look forward to when staying in Florence for a day.

**A few recommendations on things to do in Florence:**

- A symbol of Florence's architectural wonders, the **Duomo and Florence Cathedral** dominate the city's skyline. Climbing to the top of **Giotto's Bell Tower** offers gorgeous views of the city. The cathedral is known for its stunning white, pink and green marble facade and breathtaking interiors.
- Stroll along the iconic **Ponte Vecchio**, a medieval bridge spanning the breadth of the Arno River. Edged with charming shops, this unique, much-photographed bridge is not to be missed.
- Consider a visit to the **Uffizi Gallery**. Housing an unparalleled collection of Renaissance masterpieces, including works by Leonardo da Vinci, Michelangelo and Botticelli, this gallery is a haven for art enthusiasts.
- Flower lovers must not miss the **Bucolic rose garden**, home to over 350 varieties of rose and Jean-Michel Folon's bronze sculptures.
  Located near the famous vista point, **Piazzale Michelangelo**, it is a perfect spot to relax.
- The **Boboli Gardens** are an oasis of peace and tranquillity. Adjacent to the **Pitti Palace**, these gardens are home to sculptures, fountains and manicured lawns. Find a quiet spot to relax with a refreshing drink and a perhaps a picnic lunch.

- Dive into Florence's culinary scene at the **Mercato Centrale**, a bustling market in the centre of Florence. From fresh produce to local cheeses and cured meats, this market is a food lover's paradise. Sample some authentic Italian delicacies.
- Art lovers cannot miss the chance to see Michelangelo's masterpiece, 'David', housed in the **Accademia Gallery**. This iconic sculpture is one of the finest art pieces in the world.
- Explore Florence's vibrant street art scene. Local and international artists have adorned the **city's walls** with striking murals.

**How to get from the airport to the city centre:**

You will land at Florence Airport (Aeroporto di Firenze-Peretola). The best way to reach the city centre from the airport is with the Volainbus shuttle service.

Buses run every 30 minutes from the airport bus station which you will find on the right-hand side of the arrivals hall as you exit the main airport building. The journey lasts approximately 25 minutes. Purchase your ticket inside the airport at Giunti's Bookstore or directly from the bus driver.

## Milan

Milan is a radiant city, famous for fashion, art and gastronomy. Whether you are a history buff, culture vulture, foodie or sports enthusiast, this Italian metropolis offers a wide range of attractions to enjoy. Public transportation in Milan is top notch and makes visiting multiple tourist attractions in the city in a day a breeze.

**A few recommendations on things to do in Milan:**

- If in search of rest and relaxation, treat yourself to a few blissful hours at the internationally renowned **Termemilano Spa**. Ancient Spanish walls border the vast complex where 'elegant architecture blends with technology'. Just pack your swimsuit.
- **Duomo di Milano** is the city's magnificent cathedral. This Gothic masterpiece is known for its spires, statues, and intricate details. Climb to the rooftop for majestic views of Milan and the surrounding Alps.
- Art lovers will want to view Leonardo da Vinci's iconic fresco, 'The Last Supper'. Housed in **the Convent of Santa Maria delle Grazie**, this masterpiece is a testament to Da Vinci's brilliance. Make sure to book tour tickets well in advance, as entry is limited.
- Immerse yourself in Milan's artistic legacy at the **Pinacoteca di Brera**, an art gallery located in the historic Brera district. It is home to an extensive collection of Italian Renaissance art and includes works by Caravaggio, Raphael, and Bellini.

- Your next stop is the **Navigli district**. The area is known for its picturesque canals, lively markets and chic boutiques. Stroll along the waterways and sit down in one of the charming waterside cafes.
- History buffs who wish to learn more about the city's past should not miss **Sforza Castle**. This fortress is turned into a museum and houses an impressive collection of artefacts: from Michelangelo's unfinished sculptures to ancient Egyptian relics.
- No visit to Milan is complete without trying its delectable cuisine. Check out the city's food scene by exploring the **Brera district's food markets** or sampling **traditional Lombard dishes at a local trattoria**. Marry your meal up with a glass of regional wine.
- For sports enthusiasts, a visit to **San Siro Stadium** is a must. Home to both AC Milan and Inter Milan, this iconic stadium offers guided tours that take you behind the scenes.
- Shopaholics visiting Milan will not be disappointed. The **Quadrilatero della Moda** is the city's premier shopping district. From luxury boutiques to flagship stores, this area has it all.

**A day out a little further afield:**

Day trip options from Milan include the nearby scenic town of **Bergamo** where you can take a funicular to ascend a mountain as well as the further afield Italian lake resorts such as **Garda, Iseo and Como**. All can be reached by train.

### How to get to the city centre from the airport:

The main airport in Milan is Malpensa. The best way to reach the city centre is via the Malpensa Express train. This direct train line runs from the airport to the centre of the city twice per hour. Travel time is around50 minutes.

Get your tickets from the automated ticket machines. You will find these machines just before walking down the ramp to the train platform. You can also obtain a ticket from the ticket kiosks.

Another airport that budget airlines use for Milan is Milan Bergamo.

The easiest and quickest way to reach the central Milan from here is by bus. Follow the bus signs as you leave the airport. There are two companies that provide a shuttle service: the Terravision bus and the Orio shuttle. Both have 20-30 minute departures throughout most of the day and night.

Tickets can be bought on the relevant companies' websites in advance for the lowest prices, as well as from ground and on-board ticket machines.

## Portugal

## Lisbon

Lisbon is a colourful city of pastel-hued buildings. With a selection of parks and a 19th-century botanical garden, it is also one of the greenest capital cities in Europe and offers plenty for a day tripper.

**A few suggestions on how to spend a day in Lisbon:**

- This historic quarter of **Alfama** has a nostalgic feel. It boasts traditional Fado folk music and stunning views of the city. Wander through the labyrinthine alleys, discovering hidden gems and the **São Jorge Castle**.
- Admire Lisbon's architectural wonders by visiting the **Belém Tower** and the **Jerónimos Monastery**. These UNESCO World Heritage sites showcase Manueline architecture and are steeped in maritime history.
- For art lovers, the **National Tile Museum** is a must-visit. Housed in a convent, it showcases the evolution of colourful Portuguese tilework through the centuries. The intricate azulejos (decorative ceramic tiles) are not to be missed.
- Foodies will want to stop by the **Mercado da Ribeira**, also known as Time Out Market. This bustling food hall gathers the best of Lisbon's culinary scene under one roof. You should try the egg-yolk custard tartlet **Pastel de Nata**.
- Contemporary art enthusiasts should head to **MAAT (Museum of Art, Architecture,**

**and Technology**). It contains a diverse range of exhibitions at a pretty riverside location.
- If you appreciate sunsets, head to **Miradouro da Senhora do Monte**. It is a perfect place to catch stunning views of Lisbon's skyline.

## A day out a little further afield:

The fairy-tale town of **Sintra** with its elaborately decorated, yellow and red Palace is worth the trip by train. If you want to be able to claim to have visited the westernmost point in Europe and watch the powerful Atlantic Ocean crashing the rocky shore where for thousands of years Portuguese explorers believed was the end of the world, visit **Cabo da Roca**.

## Getting to the City Centre from the Airport:

Lisbon Airport, also called Humberto Delgado Airport is the main airport. The easiest way to reach the centre of the city from the airport is via the metro. The metro station of the airport is adjacent to the arrivals hall in Terminal 1.

If you land at Terminal 2, you need to take the free shuttle bus which runs between the two terminals. Journey time to the city centre via metro is about 20 minutes and trains depart every 7-10 minutes. Purchase a re-loadable Viva Viagem card which allows you unlimited rides on Lisbon public transportation (metro, trams, and buses).

## Faro

Situated on Portugal's imposing Algarve coast, charming Faro offers a mix of culture and natural beauty. Rich in historic architecture and with a vibrant local atmosphere, Faro makes for an ideal destination for a quick day trip.

**A few suggestions on how to spend a day in Faro:**

- Begin by wandering through the city's charming **Old Town**, enclosed by ancient walls. The old paved streets will lead you to architectural wonders such as the **Faro Cathedral** and the **Bishop's Palace**, affording a glimpse into Faro's rich history. Explore quaint shops, enjoy a coffee in traditional Portuguese cafés, or simply soak up the vibrant atmosphere.
- History buffs will want to pay a visit to the **Faro Archaeological Museum**. From Roman mosaics to Moorish ceramics, the museum should feature on your list of places to visit.
- Foodies visiting Faro can stop by the bustling **Mercado Municipal food market**. Here, you can sample fresh local produce, seafood and traditional Portuguese dishes. Try the grilled sardines and the popular **pastel de nata**.
- Nature lovers will find some peace and quiet at the **Ria Formosa Natural Park**. This picturesque park is located just a short boat ride from Faro. Explore the lagoons, marshlands and dunes.

- Art lovers can wander through Faro's streets adorned with vibrant murals and street art. Local and international artists have transformed the city into an **open-air gallery**, with spectacular street art around every corner of the city.
- No visit to Faro is complete without spending some time on the beach. The good news is that **Faro Island** is just a short ferry ride from the city. Enjoy the golden sandy beaches, relax under the sun and unwind with a refreshing drink or two. The tranquil surroundings provide an ideal retreat for travellers looking for a peaceful coastal experience.
- Attending a **Fado performance** in Faro makes for a memorable experience. There are a cluster of intimate venues in the city that offer traditional Fado music performances such as the **Faro's Municipal Museum** and **O Castelo Restaurant**.

**How to get from the airport to the city centre:**

Faro Airport is the main airport in the Algarve region and gets quite busy during the summer season. The best way to reach the city centre is by bus number 16. The bus trip takes around 20 minutes. These public buses run every 30 minutes from the airport. The bus station is in front of the terminal arrivals building, next to car park number 2. Bear in mind that bus tickets can only be purchased from the driver in cash.

# Albania

## Tirana

The capital of Albania, Tirana delights visitors with her profusion of colour. A few years ago, the then-mayor of the city transformed public buildings with vibrant paint shades and patterns and encouraged homeowners to follow suit. Now you can discover murals or quirky sculptures around every street corner.

Tuesdays are best avoided for a visit as many attractions close, including the Datji cable car, Bunk'Art 2 and the National History Museum.

**A few recommendations on places to visit:**

- Head to **Skanderbeg Square** in the heart of the city and find most of the following attractions skirting it.
- Spot the **statue of Skanderbeg** (Gjergj Kastrioti), the national hero on his horse. During the warmer months of the year, you may happen upon one of the frequent outdoor events such as concerts and festivals in the square and join the locals in the party atmosphere.
- Don't miss **Bunk'Art 2-** a converted nuclear bunker from Soviet times to a modern museum. Gain an insight into the regime that prevailed for 45 years under the Communist

regime. Located just south of the clock tower, it is easily identifiable by its semi-dome shape. Within the 24 small rooms read accounts of political persecutions and the tactics of the secret service to spy on citizens.

- **The National History Museum** explores Albania's history spanning several centuries.
- For a different perspective on the city, climb the **Clock Tower**. It affords a pleasing view of Skanderbeg square and the mountain backdrop beyond.
- The **Pyramid** is one of the city's most famous monuments. An intriguing structure, its pyramid-shaped façade is constructed from grey concrete. Originally a Communist-era build to commemorate a long-time communist leader of Albania.
- Walk to the **Fortress of Justinian (Tirana castle)** dating back to Byzantine times and take your pick from the many cafes and restaurants inside.
- Culture vultures should stop by **The Et'hem Bej Mosque.** The interior boasts breathtaking frescoes in the prayer hall depicting waterfalls and plants.
- The **cable car** that ascends **Datji mountain** is perhaps the biggest attraction of Tirana. Enjoy stunning mountain views on the 30-minute long ride. At the summit are a variety of activities including **mini golf** (adults and children), an extensive free play area as well as

**an obstacle course** featuring zip lines, nets and climbing ropes for adults and children (chargeable). **Horse and pony riding** is available as well as an Italian restaurant with sweeping views from the dining balcony. Plus **Bunk'Art 1 museum**

- (sister bunker to Bunk'Art 2) is located close to the base station.

### Getting from the airport to the city centre:

Tirana International Airport serves the city. Take the shuttle bus with the destination showing as 'Tirana' from the far end of the car park (approx. 4 euros) to reach the city centre from the airport. The journey time from the airport to the centre of the city is approximately 30 minutes.

Alternatively, take a yellow taxi from the airport directly to the Datji express cable car (not in the city centre) if this is the primary purpose for your trip. Expect to pay around 25 euros one way, but do agree on the price before climbing in. After descending again, catch a bus into the city centre to explore the attractions listed above should time permit.

## Central Europe

### Switzerland

#### Zurich

With an immaculately preserved old town and the largest lake in the whole of Switzerland picturesque Zurich is surrounded by the beautiful Alps.

**A few suggestions on how to spend a day in Zurich:**

- Stroll through the **Old Town**, known as **Altstadt.** This maze of narrow cobblestone streets, charming squares, and medieval buildings will transport you back in time. Marvel at the **Grossmünster**, an iconic twin-towered church dating back to the 12th century, and the **Fraumünster**, famous for its stunning stained glass windows.
- Culture vultures visiting Zurich should not miss the **Kunsthaus Zurich**. This premier art gallery displays an extensive collection of international masterpieces, from the Middle Ages to contemporary works. Also check out the **Swiss National Museum**, a fairy-tale-

like castle that is home to an assortment of artefacts that illustrate Switzerland's cultural history.
- Zurich is a foodie's paradise. Visit **Markthalle im Viadukt**, where vendors showcase their gourmet delights. Treat your taste buds to Swiss specialities such as fondue and raclette.
- Nature lovers will enjoy beautiful **Lake Zurich**. Admire her iconic **Aquaretum fountain** then take a boat ride to enjoy breathtaking views of the city and the surrounding Alps. Searching for a more active experience? Hike or bike along the **trails of Uetliberg mountain**.
- For sports fans, a visit to the **FIFA World Football Museum** is a must. Explore the history of the world's most popular sport through interactive displays and memorabilia.
- Unwind in the trendy district of **Zurich West**. Explore the vibrant street art or check out the Swiss **Federal Institute of Technology (ETH Zurich)**.
- More than 1,200 **fountains** are dotted around the city, many stunningly decorative. All provide safe, clean water to refill your water bottle.

**How to get to the city centre from the airport:**

From Zurich International Airport you can reach the city centre via the numerous train and metro lines such as S16, S2, IR75, IC5, IC1, IC8. It takes around 15 minutes to reach the centre of Zurich.

Tickets can be purchased at the machines located in the arrivals hall. Find the railway station on the underground level by following the clearly labelled signs.

## Basel

Nestled on the banks of the Rhine River, Basel is a delightful mesh of both historic and contemporary architecture. Admire unique buildings designed by some of the best architects in the world or maybe enjoy a Rhine River cruise to experience the city from a different angle.

**A few suggestions on how to spend a day in Basel:**

- Start with a visit to the **Basel Minster**, an iconic Gothic cathedral that dominates the city's skyline. Climb to the top for amazing views of the Rhine and the old town.
- The **Kunstmuseum Basel** is your next stop. Housing an impressive collection spanning from the Middle Ages to contemporary art, the museum showcases works by renowned artists such as Holbein, Van Gogh, and Picasso.
- Wander through the enchanting **Old Town**, a labyrinth of narrow streets lined with colourful

medieval buildings. Discover hidden gems, charming boutiques and welcoming cafes.
- Nature lovers can embark on a serene **Rhine river cruise**, offering breathtaking views of the city and its surroundings.
- Head to **Marktplatz**, the central square, surrounded by vibrant market stalls. For foodies, this is a culinary heaven. Try a variety of Swiss delicacies and fresh produce.
- Admire the beauty of **Rathaus (Town Hall)** with its vibrant red façade. This building is a testament to Basel's medieval charm.
- Travellers interested in contemporary design should not miss the **Swiss Architecture Museum**. Exhibitions showcasing cutting-edge architecture and urban development will leave you breathless.
- Sports fans can catch the electric atmosphere at **St. Jakob-Park**, the home stadium of FC Basel.
- If you're travelling with animal lovers, **Basel Zoo** offers a delightful experience. The zoo is home to a diverse array of animals and beautifully landscaped enclosures.

**How to get to the city centre from the airport:**

From Basel International Airport the best way to reach the city centre is by bus number 50. The buses run frequently and the total journey time is around 20 minutes. You will find the number 50 bus at the bus stands just outside the terminal building. Simply the signs that state: "Ground Transportation". Purchase tickets from the machines by the bus stands.

## Geneva

Geneva is nestled on the shores of Lake Geneva. With a chic waterfront, delicious chocolate and a picturesque old town dominated by an impressive cathedral, Geneva is a perfect destination for a quick weekend getaway trip from the UK.

**A few suggestions on how to spend a day or two in Geneva:**

- Visit **Jet d'Eau**, the iconic water fountain. It shoots water 140 metres into the air, making for a mesmerizing sight. Whether you choose to admire it from the lakeside promenade or take a boat ride for a closer look, the Jet d'Eau is a must-see attraction.
- History buffs will appreciate a visit to **St. Pierre Cathedral**, a stunning architectural marvel that dates back to the 12th century. Climb to the top for panoramic views of the city and the lake and explore the archaeological site beneath the cathedral.
- Pay a visit to the **International Red Cross and Red Crescent Museum**. Engaging

exhibits showcase the history of humanitarian aid and the organizations that call Geneva home.

- Explore the **Palais des Nations, the European headquarters of the United Nations.** Take a guided tour to discover the intricacies of international diplomacy and see attractions such as the Assembly Hall, Council Chamber and the iconic Broken Chair sculpture.
- Gee to know Geneva's **Old Town**, an area where narrow cobblestone streets wind their way through medieval buildings. Discover hidden gems like Maison Tavel, Geneva's oldest house, and explore the vibrant **Place du Bourg-de-Four.**
- Nature love will want to visit **Parc La Perle du Lac**. This tranquil park along the lake is perfect for a leisurely stroll or a peaceful picnic. Enjoy the beauty of the botanical gardens and the majestic views of the Mont Blanc mountain range.
- No visit to Switzerland is complete without enjoying its world-renowned chocolate and cheese. Join one of the **tasting tours** to sample exquisite Swiss chocolates and cheeses.
- If you're a sports enthusiast, **Lake Geneva** offers a plethora of activities. Try your hand at windsurfing and paddleboarding. Travellers can also hop on a relaxing boat cruise to soak

up the breathtaking scenery from a different perspective.

## A day out a little further afield:

To explore further afield and revel in more of Switzerland's natural beauty, visit **Montreux**. Catch the train at the airport with destination 'Brig' to reach Montreaux in just over an hour. You can buy tickets at the ticket machines and pay by card. Sit upstairs for breathtaking views over Lake Geneva and snow-capped mountains. Once at Montreaux, stroll around the lake to **Chillon castle** and enjoy the many sculptures and photo opportunities en route.

## How to get from the airport to the centre of the city:

The best way to get from Geneva International Airport to the city centre is by bus. You can hop on buses 5, 10, 28, 57, V, 5+, 23, 56 or 66 at the airport to reach different parts of the city. Bus stations for all services can be found outside of the arrivals terminal, near the arrivals car park along the Route de L'Aeroport.

The journey by bus will take around 20 minutes. Want to hear some good news? For those arriving at the airport and transiting to the city centre, the airport currently offers a free transfer ticket.

## Germany

## Berlin

Berlin is one of the most cosmopolitan cities in Europe with multiple art galleries, hip cafes, innovative dining establishments and vibrant nightclubs. Thanks to its multiculturalism, the capital of Germany is a welcoming place. It is full of historical monuments, spectacular architecture and cutting-edge art.

**A few suggestions on how to spend a day in Berlin:**

- Start your journey at the iconic **Brandenburg Gate**, a neoclassical marvel that once stood as a symbol of division during the Cold War.
- For art enthusiasts, a visit to the **East Side Gallery** is simply a must. This open-air gallery stretches along a remaining section of the Berlin Wall and is adorned with vibrant murals and graffiti.

- Dive into Berlin's cultural heritage with a visit to **Museum Island** a UNESCO World Heritage site. Museum Island consists of five renowned Berlin museums: **Alte Nationalgalerie, Altes Museum, Bodemuseum, Neues Museum, to Pergamonmuseum.** From ancient artefacts at the Pergamon Museum to the Egyptian treasures in the Neues Museum, history buffs will instantly fall in love with this area.
- Nature lovers should spend a few hours at **Tiergarten Park**. Rent a bike or take a leisurely stroll along the paths. Don't miss the picturesque **Victory Column.**
- Relive the Cold War era by visiting **Checkpoint Charlie**, the famous border crossing between East and West Berlin. The nearby museum explains the city's divided history.
- Explore the eclectic vibe of **Kreuzberg**. This neighbourhood is a melting pot of cultures, offering a mix of trendy boutiques, alternative galleries, music venues and diverse dining options. It's the ideal place to experience Berlin's alternative side.
- Explore the **Sony Centre**. Packed with dozens of commercial buildings and entertainment facilities like IMAX theatre, outdoor bars, the **Museum of Film and Television** and the **Legoland Discovery Centre.**

**Getting to the city centre from the airport:**

Brandenburg Airport is the main international airport in Berlin. The easiest way to reach the city centre is with Express trains RB14 and RE7 that depart every 30 minutes and take 30 minutes. There is also the option of taking the S-Bahn local railway route which runs every 5-20 minutes but takes 40 minutes to the centre.

The railway station is a five-minute walk from Brandenburg Airport. Purchase tickets at the airport's train station or online.

### Hamburg

Germany's second-largest city, Hamburg is known for its historic architecture, bustling harbour and innovative food scene. The city is positioned on the banks of the Elbe River and there are several esteemed museums, galleries and theatres to enjoy. It is a city of rock and roll and a place where the legendary Beatles held their earliest gigs back in the 1960's.

**A few tips on how to spend a day in Hamburg:**

- Explore Hamburg's iconic harbour, the beating heart of the city. The **Speicherstadt**, a UNESCO World Heritage Site, is a maze of red-brick warehouses lining the water's edge. Dive into the city's maritime past by taking a boat tour through the canals.
- For history enthusiasts, a visit to the **International Maritime Museum** is simply

a must. Housed in a former warehouse, this museum boasts an impressive collection of maritime artefacts, ship models and historical documents.
- As you stroll through the city, make your way to the **Kunsthalle Hamburg**, an art museum that showcases a vast array of European masterpieces spanning several centuries. From the works of Rembrandt to contemporary German artists, the **Kunsthalle** displays something to captivate every art lover.
- To tantalize your taste buds and grab a few beers, head to the **St. Pauli district**, renowned for its diverse culinary scene and alternative lifestyle. Try local specialities like **Labskaus**, a traditional sailor's dish.
- While you are in St. Pauli, don't miss the home **stadium of St. Pauli football club**. Those with a passion for this game will claim that St. Pauli is significantly more than your average football club.
- Nature lovers should plan to see the **Planten un Blomen** park, a serene oasis in the heart of the city. With vibrant flower displays, tranquil lakes and scenic walking paths, it provides a perfect escape from the urban hustle. Don't forget to catch the enchanting water light concerts that take place in the park's lake during the summer season.
- No visit to Hamburg is complete without checking out **Elbphilharmonie**, an

architectural masterpiece and a symbol of the city's cultural renaissance.

## How to get to the city centre from the airport:

The most convenient way to reach the city from Hamburg airport is via the S-Bahn line S1 train. Trains depart every 10 minutes and journey time to the Central Railway Station (Hauptbahnhof) is 25 minutes.

Tickets can be bought from vending machines at the station or online through HVV. You will find the train station underneath the arrivals Terminals 1 and 2.

## Cologne

Bustling with life and character, Cologne features medieval Romanesque churches, world-renowned museums, welcoming residents and a vibrant Belgian Quarter. This university city perched on the banks of the river Rhine radiates charm.

## A few recommendations on things to do in Cologne:

- Start centrally to explore Cologne with a visit to the iconic **Cologne Cathedral (Kölner Dom)**. Standing tall and majestic, this UNESCO World Heritage site is a masterpiece of Gothic architecture. Marvel at the intricate details of its façade and climb to the top for awesome views of the city and the Rhine River.
- For a dive into Cologne's cultural scene, proceed to **Museum Ludwig**. It houses an

impressive collection of modern art, including works by Picasso, Warhol, and Lichtenstein.
- Learn about Cologne's history with a stroll through the **Old Town (Altstadt)**. Cobblestone streets, medieval architecture, and lively squares characterise this charming area. Make sure to visit the historic **Old Market**, where you'll find the **City Hall** and the **Twelve Romanesque Churches**. The Alter Markt square, surrounded by colourful houses, is a perfect spot to relax and people watch.
- To satisfy your taste buds, explore the culinary delights on offer at **Cologne Chocolate Museum.** Discover the history of chocolate, witness the chocolate-making process and indulge in some sweet treats.
- Nature lovers can find solace in the **Rheinpark,** a pretty park set along the riverbank. Take a leisurely stroll, have a picnic or simply enjoy the serene surroundings.
- In the evening, explore the trendy **Belgian Quarter (Belgisches Viertel**). This hip neighbourhood is brimming with boutiques, cafes and bars. It is the perfect place to unwind, shop for unique finds and to sample local cuisine at one of the many charming eateries.

**Getting to the city centre from the airport:**

Cologne-Bonn airport serves Cologne. The best way to reach the city centre is by the S-Bahn train. This fast train runs frequently 24/7 and travel time is just 14 minutes. Purchase tickets online or at Cologne airport railway station's ticket machines. Travellers will find Cologne Bonn airport's train station as soon as they exit the arrival hall and can follow the clear signage.

**Eurostar train to Cologne:**

Eurostar connects London and Cologne with one quick change at Brussels-Midi/Zuid. On arrival to Brussels, just take the exit at the end of the platform down to the main hall and check the departure boards for your connecting Eurostar train to Cologne. It takes 4 hours to reach Cologne from London.

## Munich

The capital of Bavaria, Munich is a city best known for its world-famous Oktoberfest. However, there is much more to this German festival than just beer and bratwurst. This modern city is famed for its museums, historic landmarks and cultural festivals and offers an array of experiences and attractions.

**How to spend a day or two in Munich:**

- Start your Bavarian adventure at **Marienplatz**, the central square that pulses with life and history. The **Glockenspiel**, a spectacular clock tower adorned with animated figurines, puts on a delightful show at 11:00, 12:00, and 17:00.
- Nature lovers can look forward to strolling through the **Englischer Garten**, one of the

world's largest urban parks. As you meander through its lush greenery, pause at the serene **Kleinhesseloher See (Small Hessian Lake)** or watch surfers riding the artificial waves at the **Eisbachwelle.**
- For a taste of Bavarian opulence, head to **Nymphenburg Palace**. The former summer residence of Bavarian monarchs, this magnificent palace boasts splendid baroque architecture and beautifully landscaped gardens. Explore the opulent rooms, including the grand **Hall of Mirrors**.
- A haven for foodies, **Viktualienmarkt** is Munich's bustling open-air market. Sample local delights such as pretzels, sausage and cheeses, or pick up fresh produce to enjoy later. With over 140 stalls, this market is huge.
- Automobile enthusiasts will be drawn to the **BMW Welt and Museum** which provides an immersive experience into the world of Bavarian Motor Works. Admire the sleek designs, cutting-edge technology and remarkable collection of classic and contemporary BMW vehicles.
- No visit to Munich is complete without a stop at **Hofbräuhaus**, the city's most famous beer hall. Sample traditional Bavarian dishes and raise a pint of beer to the sounds of live music.
- For a touch of modernity, explore **Olympiapark,** the site of the 1972 Summer Olympics. The park's futuristic architecture,

serene lakes and panoramic views make it a delightful spot for a leisurely stroll. If you're feeling adventurous, you can even climb to the top of the Olympic Tower for magnificent views of the city.

**Getting from the airport to the city centre:**

From Munich Airport, the most efficient way to reach the city centre is via the S-Bahn S1 and S8 lines which depart every 10 minutes. However, the S8 line is considerably faster, taking only 38 minutes.

Tickets can be purchased from the S-Bahn ticket counters or the ticket machines at the airport railway station. You will find the train station on the basement level of the central area (between Terminals 1 and 2).

## Nuremberg

Located in the heart of Bavaria, Nuremberg is steeped in medieval charm. The enchanting old town is adorned with gorgeous architecture and lined with cobblestone streets.

**A few suggestions on how to spend a day in Nuremberg:**

- Your first stop is **Nuremberg Castle**, a towering fortress that offers panoramic views of the city. Explore its medieval structures, including the **Kaiserburg (Imperial**

**Castle)**, where you'll step back in time while wandering through its well-preserved rooms.
- For art enthusiasts, a visit to **Albrecht Dürer's House** is a must. The renowned Renaissance artist lived in this charming half-timbered house and today it serves as a museum showcasing his life and works.
- Stroll through the picturesque Old Town, where medieval and half-timbered buildings line the streets. **The Hauptmarkt (Main Market Square)** is a hub of activity, especially during the festive seasons.
- Nature lovers can unwind at **Tiergarten Nürnberg**, one of Germany's oldest zoos. Home to a diverse array of animals and beautifully landscaped grounds, this zoo provides a relaxing escape within the city.
- Pay a visit to **Hausbrauerei Altstadthof**, a brewery dating back to the Middle Ages. Indulge in a selection of craft beers, brewed on-site, and try delicious traditional Franconian dishes in a cosy atmosphere.
- Experience the lively atmosphere of **Nuremberg's Market Square**, surrounded by colourful buildings and bustling shops. Admire the beautiful **Frauenkirche**, a Gothic church that dominates the square. If you're visiting during the Christmas season, don't miss the famous Nuremberg **Christkindlesmarkt**.

- Visiting Nuremberg with children? Unleash your inner child at the **Toy Museum**, where a vast collection showcases the evolution of toys throughout the ages. From antique dolls to modern board games, this museum is beloved by younger visitors.

**Getting to the city centre from the airport:**

The fastest way to get to the centre of the city from Nuremberg Airport is by metro. The U-Bahn (underground) line U2 departs frequently throughout the day and takes you to the centre of the city in about 13 minutes.

Tickets can be purchased at the airport's ticket machines or online. You can reach the 'Nürnberg Flughafen' metro station easily by following the signs once you reach the arrivals hall. The station is located underground, near the airport's exit.

**Bremen**

A lively port city, Bremen is an ideal destination for a quick getaway. This cosmopolitan city on the river Weser is home to one of the most beautifully preserved historical old towns in Germany. Bursting with art and culture, this pedestrian-friendly city is packed with art galleries and museums.

**A few suggestions on how to spend a day in Bremen:**

- Fan of riverside walks? Nestled on the banks of the Weser River in the Old Town, **Schlachte** is a pedestrian zone where visitors can go for a stroll along the river. Grab a glass of Beck's beer from one of the riverside biergartens and relish the magnificent views.
- Located in the centre of Bremen's Old Town, the **Market Square (Marktplatz)** is a popular gathering spot among tourists and locals. This picturesque square is fringed by restaurants and bars situated inside historic merchant houses.
- Art lovers will want to stop by the **Kunsthalle**. The fabulous art museum in Bremen's Old Town houses a remarkable collection of Dutch, French, and German paintings dating as far back as the 14th century. Visitors will also find nearly 230,000 drawings and prints, as well as a collection of sculptures.
- With picturesque alleyways lined with wooden houses from the medieval ages, **Schnoor** is the oldest neighbourhood in the city. Lose yourself in a maze of narrow cobblestone streets where 15th-century buildings have been sympathetically transformed into galleries, boutiques and cafes.
- **Oenophiles** visiting Bremen will be keen to call in at the **Bremen Ratskeller**. This 600-year-old wine cellar contains one of the most extensive wine collections in the whole of Germany. A guided tour includes a visit to the

wine cellar and the underground storage rooms, plus wine tasting.
- Outdoor enthusiasts can go for a walk through the beautiful **Rhododendron Park**. In addition to more than 1,000 rhododendron and azalea species that bloom in the springtime, this park also has a botanical garden and a quaint 19th century windmill.
- Hop on one of the **Weser River tours** to see Bremen from a different perspective.

**Getting to the city centre from the airport:**

Tram line number 6 whisks travellers from the airport to the city centre in around 15-20 minutes. From Monday to Friday, the tram runs every 6 to 10 minutes in both directions. On Saturday, the tram departs every 10 minutes, and on Sunday every 20 minutes.

You will find the tram station (line 6) right in front of terminal A. The station has 2 vending machines where you can purchase tram tickets.

## Baden-Baden

Baden-Baden is one of Europe's most notable spa towns and was built on thermal springs. Located near the French border, this picturesque town in southwest Germany boasts refined architecture, a scenic funicular ride and offers a range of spa treatments.

**A few suggestions on how to spend a day in Baden-Baden:**

- Journey through time by exploring the **Roman Bath Ruins and Museum**. Wander through the well-preserved remains of Roman baths dating back to the 2nd century AD.
- For the culture vultures, a visit to **Festspielhaus**, one of Europe's largest opera houses, is a must. Experience the world of classical music, ballet and opera and witness performances by world-renowned artists inside an intricately decorated venue.
- Nature lovers can ascend the iconic **Merkur Mountain** via a scenic funicular ride. The panoramic views from the summit offer a breathtaking perspective of the Black Forest. Hike along well-marked trails or have a memorable dining experience at the mountaintop restaurant.
- Indulge in the epitome of relaxation at **Caracalla Spa**, where thermal waters with healing properties have been attracting visitors for centuries. From soothing thermal baths to luxurious spa treatments, the modern spa complex offers a range of wellness experiences.
- Stroll along the enchanting **Lichtentaler Allee**, a picturesque park dotted with centuries-
- For a touch of glamour, try your luck at the **Baden-Baden Casino**, one of the oldest and most opulent casinos in Europe.
- Admire the architectural beauty of **Kurhaus**, a majestic building located in the heart of the

town. The surrounding gardens are also worth a look.
- Art lovers will want to visit the **Museum Frieder Burda**. Expect to find a remarkable collection of modern and contemporary art.
- Thrill seekers could enjoy a day at **Europa Park**, Germany's largest and most popular theme park. With impeccable theming based on European countries there are attractions for all ages plus **Rulantica**, a huge indoor water park. Take a taxi or hire car from the airport and arrive there in 45 minutes.

**Getting to Baden-Baden city centre from the airport:**

Karlsruhe/ Baden-Baden Airport serves the city. To reach the city centre, take the Baden-Airpark Express Bus number 285. Bus tickets are available from the ticket vending machine at the bus stop in front of the terminal. The journey typically takes around 30 minutes and buses leave the airport every hour between early morning and 23:20.

## Austria

### Vienna

Austria's capital features Baroque architecture, glittering palaces and world-famous museums with fabled art collections. From trying the famous Viennese cakes and pastries to visiting some of the best museums in Europe, there is much to appreciate.

**A few suggestions on how to spend a day in Vienna:**

- The **Museumsquartier** in Vienna is a mecca for culture vultures and history buffs. See works by Gustav Klimt and Oskar Kokoschka, as well as Schiele paintings at the **Leopold Museum**. To admire the masterpieces by Andy Warhol, go to the **Museum of Modern Art**. The **Museumsquartier Wien, or MQ** is also an area packed with rooftop terraces, trendy bars, cafes and fine dining establishments.
- Once a residence of the Hapsburgs (rulers of the Austrian empire), **Schönbrunn Palace** is one of the most popular tourist attractions in Vienna. Allow 3+ hours to view the palace and its manicured grounds. Book your tour beforehand and see the interiors of one of the most impressive palaces in Europe.
- There is also the spectacular **Hofburg Palace** where the Habsburgs used to spend their winter days. Today, the palace is home to the president of Austria. There are three museums that you can visit here: the **Imperial Silver Collection**, the **Sisi Museum** (crown jewels), and the **Imperial Apartments**.
- Welcome to **Prater**, a popular amusement park in Austria. It is home to the world-famous **Riesenrad**, a 65-metre-high Ferris wheel built in the 19th century. Brave thrilling rides, as

well as one of the oldest ghost trains in the world. Entrance to the Prater is free of charge!
- Built in the 19th century, the **Vienna State Opera House** is one of the largest theatres in the world. See the grand staircase and the magnificent Tea Room and its tapestries.
- Foodies should try the signature cake, **Saschetorte**. It is a perfect combination of apricot jam, chocolate sponge and dark chocolate ganache. Travellers will find versions of this beloved sweet treat in cafes across the city.

**Getting to the city from the airport:**

The best way to get to the city centre from Vienna airport is by train. The train station is right under the terminal, a 5-minute walk from the arrivals. The City Airport Train (CAT) directly links the airport and the Wien Mitte station.

Purchase your ticket from the ticket machines with cash or a card at the airport train station. The journey takes 16 minutes and trains run every few minutes.

## Innsbruck

Innsbruck is a small city in the Tyrol region of Austria known for its charming old streets, breathtaking viewpoints and internationally acclaimed museums.

**A few suggestions on how to spend a day in Innsbruck:**

- Locally known as the **Altstadt, the Old Town** of Innsbruck has plenty of well-preserved medieval houses in the narrow streets. Stroll around to find some of the finest examples of Renaissance, Baroque and old Tyrolese architecture.
- Located in the Old Town, the **Imperial Palace** is an unmissable attraction in the city. Go on a walking tour of the palace to see the beautiful **Baroque Helblinghaus** and the 57-meter-high **Stadtturm medieval watchtower**. After climbing the 133-step staircase, travellers will be rewarded with magnificent 360-degree views of Innsbruck.
- The main tourist and shopping street, **Maria-Theresien-Strasse** is lined with gorgeous 17th- and 18th-century houses. Stroll along this pedestrian street to find attractions like the **Town Hall** and **St. Anne's Column**.
- A superb museum that focuses on fine arts from late prehistoric times to the present day, The **Tyrolean State Museum** is an amazing place to visit.
- Glean an understanding of Tyrolean life in days gone by at the **Tyrolean Folk Art Museum**. Displays are presented in English language.
- Learn about the history, politics and religion in Tirol at the **Tirol Panorama**.
- Stop by the amazing **Visual Museum** which is dedicated to mysterious and marvellous optical illusions.

- **Nordkette** is the closest mountain to Innsbruck. For jaw-dropping mountain scenery and panoramic views of the city, ride the **Hungerburgbahn funicular** to the Innsbruck suburb of Hungerburg.
- To venture a little further afield, take the train to **Feste Kufstein**, a charming Tirolese border town best known for its medieval castle, fortress and historic fountains and monuments.

**How to get from the airport to the city centre:**

Innsbruck Airport is close to the city centre. Take the bus route F from the airport. The bus departs every 15 minutes and brings you to the central station (to Innsbruck Hauptbahnhof) in 20 minutes. However, get off the bus at Anichstraße/Rathausgalerien instead (a station that is closer to the old town).

Find the bus stop directly outside the terminal. Bear in mind that the bus only operates every 30 minutes in the evening, on Sundays and during public holidays. Tickets can be bought online or from ticket machines. You can also buy a ticket directly from the driver, but it costs extra.

## Poland

### Warsaw

Located on the Vistula River, Warsaw is famed for its medieval architecture, exquisite palaces and eye-catching old town. The capital of Poland can be easily explored in a day or two thanks to the city's reliable public transport.

## A few suggestions on how to spend a day in Warsaw:

- Start your day in Warsaw with a visit to the **Royal Castle**. Located in **Castle Square**, this UNESCO World Heritage site once served as the residence of Polish monarchs. Explore the opulent chambers, marvel at the extensive art collection and take in sweeping views of the city from the castle grounds.
- For a taste of royal extravagance, head out to **Wilanów Palace**. Surrounded by beautifully manicured gardens, this Baroque masterpiece is often referred to as the "Polish Versailles." Wander through the lavishly decorated rooms and admire the beauty of picturesque gardens.
- Delve into the intricate history of Polish Jews at the **Polin Museum**. Through immersive exhibits, the museum takes you on a journey through 1000 years of the history of Polish Jews.
- Take a leisurely stroll through Warsaw's charming **Old Town**, a UNESCO World Heritage site. Admire the meticulously reconstructed buildings, each with its unique story and indulge in the vibrant local culture.
- Nature lovers will want to visit **Łazienki Park**, Warsaw's largest public park. Roam through the serene landscape, visit the **Palace**

**on the Isle** and catch a glimpse of the iconic Chopin Monument. In the summer, attend open-air Chopin concerts.

- Sample traditional Polish foods: pierogi (dumplings), gołąbki (cabbage rolls), bigos (sauerkraut and meat stew) and kiełbasa (Polish sausage).
- Sports fans can pay a visit to the **National Stadium (Stadion Narodowy)**. Catch a game or simply tour the impressive structure that hosted the UEFA Euro 2012.
- In the afternoon, go for a walk to the **Neon Museum.** It is a homage to the vibrant neon signs that once adorned Warsaw's streets.

**Getting to the City Centre from the Airport:**

Chopin Airport is the busiest airport in Poland. The easiest way to reach the city centre from the airport is by bus. There are two bus routes that connect the airport to the downtown area: 175 and 188. Buses run every 20 to 30 minutes and the journey time is approximately 25 minutes depending on the traffic.

The brand-new bus station is located on the arrivals terminal level. Purchase your tickets at the passenger information point in the arrivals hall.

## Krakow

Krakow is a culturally rich city known for its medieval architecture, Jewish quarter and vibrant nightlife. This vibrant city in Southern Poland is compact in size, making it easy to visit the many popular attractions on foot.

## A few suggestions on how to spend a day in Krakow:

- Visit the iconic **Wawel Castle and Cathedral**. Perched on a hill, this architectural marvel boasts centuries of Polish royal history. Explore the stunning interiors and admire views of the Vistula River.
- Step into the beating heart of Krakow, the iconic **Rynek Główny**. This expansive square is the largest medieval market square in Europe and is surrounded by colourful townhouses and charming cafes to sit and people watch in.
- Discover Krakow's cultural diversity in **Kazimierz, the Jewish Quarter**. Wander through its narrow streets adorned with street art and visit historic synagogues. The district is also home to trendy cafes, art galleries and a thriving nightlife scene.
- For the foodies, a trip to Poland is incomplete without trying **pierogi** – traditional Polish dumplings. From classic potato and cheese to more adventurous combinations like spinach and feta, there are many versions of pierogi that you can try while staying in Krakow for a day or two. Also try **zurek**, a hearty soup served inside a hollowed-out loaf of bread.

- Escape the urban bustle and take a stroll through picturesque **Planty Park**. It offers a peaceful retreat with its gardens, sculptures and benches.
- Enjoy a scenic **Wisła River cruise**. Relax on a boat, admire the city's skyline and observe the city's attractions from the water.

**A day out a little further afield:**

On an overnight trip consider booking a private tour online to drive you to the **Wieliczka salt mine** to explore the amazing chambers and natural sculptures. It is also possible to visit **Auschwitz-Birkenau**, the largest Nazi WW2 concentration camp, for a sobering tour from Krakow. Most tour companies include both destinations in a full day of approximately 11 hours.

**Getting to the city centre from the airport:**

From John Paul II International Airport Kraków–Balice, take the bus number 208 which runs every hour and stops at Krakow central station. Alternatively, number 252 runs every 30 minutes but stops at the southern side of ICE Congress Centre. After 23:00, take the 902-night bus.

The bus stops are just outside the airport terminal. Purchase tickets from machines next to the bus station or onboard the bus.

### **Slovenia**

## Ljubljana

Ljubljana is the charming capital of Slovenia. This hidden gem is crammed with interesting and varied architecture. Equally as stunning as her neighbour Croatia, Slovenia offers excellent value for money.

**A few suggestions on how to spend a day in Ljubljana:**

- Visit **Preseren Square**, named after Slovenia's greatest poet, France Preseren. This lively square is surrounded by elegant baroque buildings and is dominated by the iconic pink **Franciscan Church**. Take a moment to admire the **Triple Bridge**, a unique architectural masterpiece.
- **Ljubljana Castle** is a must-visit. The medieval fortress sits atop **Castle Hill**, offering panoramic views of the city. Explore the castle's museum to uncover the city's history.
- To satisfy your cultural cravings, visit the **National Gallery of Slovenia**. Housed in an impressive Neo-Renaissance palace, it showcases an extensive collection of Slovenian art. The nearby **Museum of Modern Art** is perfect for contemporary art enthusiasts.
- Continue your journey along the Ljubljanica River, where you will find the vibrant **Central Market**. Here, the stalls are teeming with

fresh produce, handmade crafts and local delicacies.
- Look out for the winged beasts keeping watch on the famous **Dragon Bridge** in Ljubljana.
- Nature lovers can spend a few hours at **Tivoli Park**, a green haven in the heart of the city. Wander along scenic paths, enjoy the blooming flowers or just relax and people-watch.
- Located just a short walk from the park, the local **Union Brewery** offers reasonably priced guided tours of the brewery and has a taproom where travellers can feast on local foods and imbibe in a pint of fresh Union beer.

**A day out a little further afield:**

If you are staying in the city for an extra day or two, visit captivating **Lake Bled** and admire the beauty of the emerald-green waters. Ride on a traditional pletna boat to the tiny Bled Island.

**Getting to the city centre from the airport:**

Ljubljana Jože Pučnik Airport is the main international airport in Slovenia. The easiest way to reach the city centre is on the Alpetour bus No. 28. Buses depart regularly and the journey to the city centre takes about 45 minutes depending on the traffic.

You can purchase your ticket directly from the bus driver. The Alpetour bus can be found in front of the airport terminal.

# Part Three: 50 Bonus Travel Tips

## 50 Bonus Travel Tips

1. Join the Extreme Travel UK Facebook group. The ultimate inspiration for day and overnighter trips abroad with countless trip reviews from people who have visited places you may be considering visiting plus others you may not have even heard of. They are a friendly bunch but out of courtesy do try a search for information in the group before posting and a simple 'please' or 'thank you' is appreciated when asking others to spare time to help you.

2. Carry a mobile battery power bank charger in case your phone needs charging on the go. It could prove invaluable in the case of delays.

3. Ensure you have plenty of data available on your phone before your trip and make the most of for any free Wi-Fi availability on public transport as well as in cafes etc.

4. Contact your bank ahead of time to let them know you will be using your card abroad.

5. When packing, have any electronic devices such as phones and hair straighteners

accessible at the top of your bag so you can easily remove them at security.

6. Before booking a flight, always check how far the destination airport is from the city centre. Some take over an hour to reach, which cuts significantly into your exploring time.

7. For a huge amount of information on train travel throughout Europe, check out seat61.com. Comprehensive information is available on booking international night trains as well as rail options from destination airports to explore further afield.

8. After returning from a day trip to a destination city, rather than forgetting about that location once it has been ticked off, how about exploring other towns or resorts accessible by an hour (or so)'s train journey? To name just one example, Montreux in Switzerland can be reached from Geneva in an hour and is worth it for the breathtaking scenery from the train alone. Seat61.com is ideal to explore your options.

9. Food served on the low-cost airlines is overpriced. One option is to purchase a 'meal deal' lunch in one of the airside shops (for example from 'Boots') comprising a salad or

sandwich, snack and soft drink. Once consumed, the bottle can be refilled at your destination to save further costs.

10. Overnight ferries are worth exploring to make the most of an overnight trip as sleeping on the move maximises your waking hours and opens the opportunity to experience a second destination. The Helsinki to Estonia route is a popular one but a little research should discover many other routes, for instance between southern Sweden and Poland Rome to Sardinia (Olbia). Try directferries.co.uk for ideas.

11. Midweek flights on budget airlines (Tuesday to Thursday) are usually priced significantly lower than weekend flights. If can make use of these days to travel, then do.

12. Street food in most destinations is a fitting option for quick mealtimes: sample delicious local cuisine for a budget price.

13. Checking the opening times and days of preferred places of interest in advance offers reassurance that you will get to see them. Some close on one or two days each week. However, other travellers prefer to take a take-it-as-it-comes approach and enjoy allowing their day to unfold naturally.

14. Many European cities offer fantastic free walking tours led by local guides keen to impart their wealth of knowledge about their city's history and culture. Advance booking is essential. Remember to tip whatever you feel is a fair price to the guide at the end.

15. Avoid tourist traps: steer clear of restaurants or bars near major tourist sites as prices tend to be inflated and the food often of inferior quality.

16. Use public transport: Buses and trains are significantly cheaper than taxis or car rentals except in the case of larger groups of four or more.

17. If staying overnight, remember to bring an adapter plug for mainland European power sockets as theirs are incompatible with UK plugs on hair straighteners, phone chargers etc.

18. Tap water is safe to drink throughout Europe but the taste varies widely. Consider taking a mini squeezy bottle of Robinson's squash to add a few flavoured drops to make it more palatable. Ensure you add the mini squash bottle to a clear plastic bag through airport security.

19. Many museums and art galleries have a free entry day once each month. Should you be able

to time your trip with when it happens it can prove a real budget saver.

20. Booking tickets to attractions in advance, even as little as an hour before arrival can shave money off the entry cost and a fast-track entry queue is often available for advance ticket buyers to beat the crowds.

21. Set aside funds in a bank account or on a credit card to be able cover alternate flights or a hotel room in a worst case scenario.

22. Take a small pack of standard painkillers (ibuprofen or paracetamol) in their original packaging to nip headaches in the bud. Plasters are useful as walking through airports alone racks up thousands of steps and cause blisters. No need to let minor ailments spoil the day.

23. Plan rest stops throughout the day to combat tiredness. Rest stops provide the perfect opportunity to sit down with a drink, get the vibe of a place and enjoy a little people watching.

24. Check the weather forecast a day or two ahead. If it is likely to be hot, leave a bottle of suncream out the night before to remind you to apply it in the early morning. Rain need not put a dampener (sorry!) on your trip: have a pair of waterproof trousers at the ready. Although

distinctly unglamorous, they are underrated for preventing soaked-leg misery. Along with a hooded, weatherproof coat you will be ready to face the elements and still enjoy yourself.

25. Avoid buying advance timed entry tickets to attractions as unforeseen delays can render them wasted. It is safer to purchase an all-day ticket.

26. The latest flight of the day home is usually the best bet. It means less pressure to rush to the airport and often the airport will be quieter with fewer queues later into the evening. In addition, you may get the chance to experience a taste of your city by night for an alternative perspective.

27. Double check all information yourself before you travel as things are subject to change. It is great to gain ideas from travel blogs and trip reports but always confirm the details on official websites as the most up-to-date information sources.

28. Ensure that data roaming will be included on your mobile phone in your destination. Particularly in non-EU countries such as Switzerland using your phone could prove extremely costly without it. Purchasing a cheap pay-as-you-go SIM card from a network provider for as little as £10 could work out as a

better value choice. Just remember to swap back SIM cards on the flight.

29. Download the Google Translate app to your phone. You can snap a picture of a sign or menu and translate it into English almost instantly.

30. To immerse yourself into your destination ahead of time, think about learning a few basic phrases in the local language. A YouTube search should find guides on how to master them with an authentic accent and if you want to take it a step further you could download the free Duolingo app to learn more of the language.

31. Note down password prompts for your airline login and email account to keep in your wallet in case you find yourself logged out and need urgent access.

32. Download your electronic boarding passes to save on your phone and/ or print them off in case of airline app faults. A minority of destination airports insist on printed boarding passes for the return journey (e.g. Tirana).

33. If your destination airport is very small, wait a while before joining the security queue to fly home. There is often little in the way of shops to browse or other facilities to pass the time,

and boredom can set in unless you have a decent book to lose yourself in. Once you know you are safely at the airport in good time and can see that the security queues are short, browse the shops on that side first.

34. Take photos or scans of important documents such as your passport main page as a backup in case they become lost or stolen. Email them to yourself.

35. Local grocery stores can almost be an adventure in themselves-they offer valuable insight into local culture while being great places to stock up on cheap snacks.

36. Consider travelling in low season. Prices for flights and hotels often tend to be cheaper due to lower demand so you could bag a bargain as well as benefitting from fewer crowds.

37. Wear comfortable footwear. Do not underestimate the impact that walking long distances through airports and a new city can have on the feet. Flat soles are the best choice for travel days.

38. Look up the custom for tipping in your chosen destination to avoid getting it wrong and risking embarrassment in cafes and restaurants.

39. Use the 'Flush' app to locate the nearest toilets to your current location- this can prove very useful, especially if travelling with children.

40. Bring a small handy pack of tissues to act as toilet paper if necessary.

41. Stay patient. Life is too short to give rise to anger and annoyance whenever small things go wrong. Just shrug your shoulders and move on. You may even look back and laugh at the mishaps.

42. Take photos as souvenirs. Do not spend too long doing so though as being present and relishing the view in person is important too.

43. Try side streets near the tourist spots to find better value and more authentic restaurants. If they are full of locals, that's a great sign.

44. Sample the local food delicacies, often on sale from street vendors. If these are not obvious then a quick internet search will let you know what to hunt for.

45. Research the cheapest car parking options for your nearest airport. Justpark.com and holidayextras.com are two of the most popular places to source good value airport parking for a day or two, often at nearby hotels.

46. On a PC or laptop, open Google Maps to create a map of your destination city and add pins to mark all the places of interest you hope to see, as well as the railway station or bus stop. Get creative and theme it with different coloured pins to represent restaurants, attractions, transport etc. It can later be opened on your phone to enable you to see in real time the distances between places of interest etc.

47. Treat yourself to an eye mask, ear plugs and consider a travel pillow. These facilitate decent quality rest on a plane which can be invaluable on a long day of travel. If you leave your seat in the upright position and seat belt on, the cabin crew are unlikely to disturb your rest.

48. Delays of three hours plus based on flight arrival time could entitle you to compensation, should it be the airline's fault. Some suggest snapping a photo of the time in a wider shot of the open plane door as you alight as evidence when submitting a claim.

49. Use the wonderful website Rome2Rio.com to help plan journeys. Simply type in any 2 locations worldwide and it will instantly list all the ways to get there as well as a rough idea of cost. This can be particularly useful should a taxi be the most practical option for part of your trip. However, do obtain firm quotes from

the information in the search results rather than assuming the prices are entirely accurate.

50. Go with the flow if the chance of an unexpected experience presents itself. Nothing compares to the delight of discovering a street festival is taking place as you arrive or being handed free tickets to an open air music concert on a summer's evening (both of the above have happened to me). Such experiences forge memories that last a lifetime.

## Conclusion

**Time to book and experience your first European Day Trip**

I hope that by now you are teeming with anticipation at the prospect of your next trip abroad. Perhaps you have compiled a mental shortlist of a few destinations and are ready to get researching and booking one. If you live within reach of an airport, your eyes may have been opened to the wealth of opportunities for travel without a pile of money or ample free time being prerequisites. I sincerely hope that readers with less travel experience have had their confidence and knowledge levels topped up and will take the leap of going ahead with a first trip.

**The impact of EDTs on the environment**

The environmental issue may have crossed your mind at some point while reading this book and you may be wondering how much of an impact day tripping abroad has on the planet? It would be remiss of me to decline to address it.

Firstly, the surge in popularity of EDTs does not necessarily equate to additional carbon emissions. Anecdotally, a significant percentage of people have been financially impacted by the steeply increasing cost of package holidays abroad since the pandemic. Finances only permit them to replace their previously longer duration (and sometimes longer haul) holidays with the same number of (budget-friendly) smaller day trips or overnighters. Day trippers do not necessarily take any more flights than before but rather intend to stay for shorter durations.

However, short-haul flights within Europe by their very nature result in fewer emissions than long-haul flights. In addition, most flights being taken by day trippers are on budget airlines without a first-class section. This is positive because the more people that are seated on a plane, the lower the carbon footprint. The European low-cost carriers also tend to fly newer planes (Ryanair claims the average age of its plane is under 9 years) which produce fewer carbon emissions.

Thanks to constantly improving technology and sustainable aviation fuels (SAFs) carbon emission rates are improving all the time. The 'Net Zero 2050: New Aircraft Fact Sheet' by iata.org claims that: 'Each new generation of plane has reduced emissions by around 15-20%. The overall fuel efficiency of the fleet is around 80% better than 50 years ago'.

The research conducted while drafting this book brought into focus how prohibitively expensive train travel is in the UK, not to mention frustratingly unreliable with frequent cancellations and postponements which is in stark contrast to the dependable and modern railway networks present in much of continental Europe. The cost of a return flight to an exciting European city from and back to London is often lower than a one-way train journey between two English cities such as London to Manchester. Until significant investments are made to bring the standards of quality (including as a bare minimum, a seat for every paying passenger) and price of train travel in the UK in line with the superior systems abroad, the many individuals who would otherwise be keen to explore other parts of their own country will vote with their feet and hop across to the continent.

Public transportation is much promoted within this book as a means of reaching destination cities from the airport (as well as venturing further afield) as it tends to be frequent and high quality in European cities.

Holidaying in the UK is often purported as an eco-friendly choice compared to venturing abroad but this is questionable given that driving your own car both to the destination as well as on daily outings (due to costly and poor public transport availability) is necessary.

Many of us already make daily decisions that reduce our impact on the planet: sorting recyclable waste at home, reducing meat consumption and living in smaller homes than previous generations. Ultimately, we must each be answerable to our own conscience.

One practical suggestion for anyone wishing to take a step towards counteracting the impact of each flight they take is 'carbon offsetting'. Many airlines offer an option during the booking process to donate to a programme. This could include tree planting as well as broader projects such as investing in and increasing accessibility to renewable energy sources.

**To close**

Let us end with a quote: "For my part, I travel not to go anywhere, but to go. I travel for travel's sake. The great affair is to move" by Robert Louis Stevenson.

Who am I to disagree? Though I would add that personally, a significant part of the joy of travel is the sense of anticipation leading up to it. The researching of what to expect in terms of culture, language, edible delicacies, must-see attractions as well as lesser-known hidden gems.

How fortunate we are in Europe to be able to savour that sweet sense of anticipation each time we venture as little as an hour into foreign lands with the possibility of returning home to our own bed the very same evening. Americans and Australians are quick to point out just how much cultural diversity exists in a relatively small area within the continent of Europe and how enviably accessible it all is.

The majority of European cities can be reached within a mere three and a half hours; something that is all too easy to take for granted when you happen to live on the doorstep. A hankering to explore exotic lands that are a long, costly flight away is understandable, but it makes sense to instead focus on the low-hanging and just as delicious fruits that happen to be a mere stone's throw away.

**A Note from the Author**

Thank you for taking the time to read this book. It was a true pleasure to write. I hope that you enjoyed reading it and have gained some useful tips on booking and enjoying a day trip abroad.

When you have a moment (ideally right now while it is fresh in your mind, pretty please) I would be so grateful if you could write a review on Amazon: just a few short words would be perfect. For new authors like me, reviews count for a lot and will also help others like you to discover the delights that day tripping in Europe has to offer.

Best wishes,

Sarah

P.S. Please also check out the travel planner to accompany this book: **'European Day Trip Planner and Journal'**. It serves as an invaluable tool to gather all your ideas together and plan the details of your upcoming day trips. Furthermore, it will help you to commemorate the details after each journey as dedicated spaces have been provided for post-trip reflections and reviews.

It is available on Amazon in paperback.

Printed in Great Britain
by Amazon